Fearless Intelligence

The Extraordinary Wisdom of Awareness

by Michael Benner

Fearless Intelligence

The Extraordinary Wisdom of Awareness

by Michael Benner

For special discounts on bulk orders, please contact:

The Ageless Wisdom Mystery School
PO Box 6894 La Quinta, CA 92248 USA
(818) 900-AWMS (2967)
MB@MichaelBenner.com

FIRST EDITION

ISBN: 978-1-54394-249-1

People Are Talking about *Fearless Intelligence* –

"Your programs have always been a source of inspiration for me. I'm always amazed by how much focus and clarity and renewal come from just a few minutes of what you have to say."
— Recording artist Jackson Browne

"Imagine recognizing fear as an alert — not to danger, but rather to unawareness and confusion. When you release your resistance to heartache and anxiety, awareness expands and understanding replaces hurt and tension. Now stop imagining, and let Michael Benner prove to you that a fearless life is your right as a conscious human being."
— Guy Finley, author of *"The Secret of Letting Go"*

"Michael has extended his legacy with this sweeping integration of his life's lessons about love and fear — at once a memoir and a grand synthesis of psychology, neuroscience, and consciousness research."
— Connie Zweig, Ph.D., co-author of *"Meeting the Shadow"*

"Michael Benner is an embodiment of and expertly humane guide to, 'Fearless Intelligence.' This is a brave, beautifully written, illumined book that will inspire you to a richer, deeper and far more empowered life."
— Andrew Harvey, author of *"The Hope – A Guide to Sacred Activism"*

"This is the self-awareness book so many of us have been looking for. 'Fearless Intelligence' tells us how to use our personal heartache and anxiety to map and explore our undiscovered Self. As Awareness illumines the shadows within us, spiritual Love and Understanding replace fear and confusion. With practice, we climb the Spiral Path, ever closer to the Infinite Source of All That Is."
— Dave Davies, founder of the Kinks and author of *"Heal: A Guide to Meditation"*

"'Fearless Intelligence' has inspired me to have the courage and wisdom to explore my fears. It is an aspect I have pondered before, but reading this book has touched my heart to really go for it — encouraging me to be Fearless, to climb the next mountain because I know I will find the Beauty of ME."
— Ginger Gilmour, author of *"Memoirs of the Bright Side of the Moon"*

ACKNOWLEDGMENTS

My first teachers in the Personal Development field were José Silva, founder of the Silva Mind Control Method and his instructors, Ken McCauley and John Magera. In 1974, four years after graduating from Michigan State University, I took Silva's 40-hour training in Detroit. Two years later, I repeated it in Santa Monica. I also interviewed all three men several times on my radio talk shows in Detroit, Long Beach and Los Angeles.

I was so impressed with the extraordinary benefits of the Silva Method — essentially, deep relaxation, guided imagery and affirmation of goals — that I dedicated my career as a broadcast journalist and radio talk show host to picking the brains of scientists, researchers, teachers, experts and authors who were leaders in the fields of Personal and Transpersonal Development or, in some related way, truly inspiring individuals.

Since the mid-1980s, I have also enjoyed teaching, training, counseling, mentoring and coaching thousands of individuals. I offer this book as both a journalist and perpetual student of the world's mystical traditions, but make no claims to be any sort of guru or esoteric master.

A short list of my most memorable radio guests includes: Richard Bach, Gary Zukav, Marilyn Ferguson, Vernon Howard, Guy Finley, Sol Lewis, Mitch Horowitz, Andrew Harvey, Jon Kabat-Zinn, Frances Moore Lappé, Dr. Fred Alan Wolf, Michael Talbot, Dr. Ivan Barzakov, Stephan A. Schwartz, Dick Sutphen, Allen Ginsberg, Albert Hoffman, Dr. Oscar Janiger, Dr. Shafica Karagulla, Dr. Connie Zweig, Norman Cousins, Dennis Merritt Jones, Betty Bethards, Ramsey Clark, Daniel Sheehan, Ralph Nader, Paul Watson, Frank Wilkinson, Martin Sheen, Steve Allen, Dr. Michael Samuels, Adelaide Bry, Shakti Gawain, Dan Millman, Col. David Hackworth, Lt. Col. Jim Channon, Lynn Andrews, Michael Glickman, Philip Goldberg, Joseph Chilton Pearce, Lama Surya Das, Dr. Larry Dossey, Dr. David Bressler, F.M. Esfandiary (FM-2030), Dr. Wilson Bryan Key, Dr. Harold C. Urey, Dr. J. Allen Hynek, Peter Russell, James Redfield, J. Donald Walters, Don Miguel Ruiz, Laura Huxley, Paul Krassner, Ginger Gilmour, Jackson Browne, Stevland Morris (Stevie Wonder), Dr. Timothy Leary and Robert Anton Wilson.

Others who have influenced me greatly are too numerous to list, though I am compelled to acknowledge the instruction and insight provided by the published work of: Manly P. Hall, Dr. Ernest Holmes, Alan Watts, Dr. Milton H. Erickson, Erich Fromm, R. Buckminster Fuller, Dr. Martin Luther King Jr., Thich Nhat Hanh, Alice A. Bailey, Dr. Roberto Assagioli, Dr. Carl Jung, Mohandas K. Gandhi, D.T. Suzuki, Thomas Merton, Paramahansa Yogananda, Evelyn Underhill, Neville Goddard, Roy H. Jarrett, William Walker Atkinson, William James, Ralph Waldo Emerson, Dr. Thomson J. Hudson, Emile Coué, Swami Vivekananda, Jakob Böhme, Meister Eckhart and Jalaluddin Rumi.

Finally, my most sincere gratitude goes to Georgia Lambert and Lucille Cedarcrans for introducing me to theosophy and mysticism in a classroom setting; to my first mind science teacher, José Silva, founder of the Silva Mind Control Method; to Kody Bateman, Jordan Adler and Mark Herdering from Send Out Cards for revealing the heart and soul of relationship management; to my friends Cindy Spring and Felicity Artemis for patiently introducing me to the powerful dynamics of feminism; to Lieutenant Rich Meier of the Orange County Sheriff's Department, whose request for a self-awareness training for law enforcement officers led to this book; to Michael Bellah, a friend and fellow traveler since middle school for his supportive critiques; to Hannah V. Miller, a dear, lifelong friend and dedicated Montessori teacher for her editorial scrutiny; to Craig Leener, my primary editor for his vital support; to my friend Eric Lee Martin, who designed the cover and formatted this book, and to Steven Snyder, my spiritual brother, business partner for 40 years and one of the smartest, most well-read people I know. It's unlikely this book would have been completed without Steven's enduring help and support.

I am most grateful to my wife and best friend, Doreen Key, who shares my vision, encourages me and loves me without condition. Thank you for your editing, notes, spiritual guidance and the countless hours you gave me to write this book. You make love real.

"Fearlessness is not only possible, it is the ultimate joy.
When you touch non-fear, you are free."
— Thich Nhat Hanh

"What men fear is what really instructs them and
so leads finally to their liberation."
— Paul Foster Case

"When you realize that you are not the person, but the pure and
calm witness, and that fearless awareness is your very being, you are
the Being. It is the Source, the inexhaustible Possibility."
— Sri Nisargadatta Maharaj

"Going beyond fear begins when we examine our fear: our anxiety,
nervousness, concern, and restlessness. … When we slow down, when we
relax with our fear, we find sadness, which is calm and gentle…
That is the first tip of fearlessness, and the first sign of real warriorship."
— Chögyam Trungpa Rinpoche

TABLE OF CONTENTS

PREFACE

Ignorance incites fear, anger and hatred, which fortify ignorance.
Fearless Intelligence is peaceful and loving —
the extraordinary wisdom of awareness.

Fearless Intelligence is expanded awareness — the insight and understanding that become apparent in peaceful, loving states of mind. As the intelligence of fearlessness, Awareness is serene, innate wisdom. It is goodness, truth and beauty — the magical elixir and essence of Life.

This **Fearless Intelligence** book contains personal skills to develop self-awareness, self-worth and self-realization. Plus, it includes social skills to enhance empathy, compassion, respect and trust of others.

Because everything is in flux, there will always be new fears to confront. Learning to manage that personal fear, anxiety and stress not only mitigates confusion and unawareness, but provides elevated perspectives and expanded horizons.

The word *fearless* in this book does *not* refer to a denial, rejection or absence of fear. Instead of impulsively resisting anxiety or even attempting to overcome it, the reader will learn to uncover its beneficial significance. **Fearless Intelligence** provides practical tools to reverse the devastating effects of fear on awareness, and consequently develop comprehension, reasoning, intuitive insight and understanding.

Besides *awareness*, other terms for **Fearless Intelligence** include higher consciousness, self-realization, intuitive intelligence, insight, metacognition, understanding, enlightenment, mindfulness and wisdom. In a spiritual sense, Love also refers to the edified insight that becomes available as we study our fear. Awareness is the supreme quality of mind, and Love is the wisdom of the heart — two sides of the same coin.

As a result of sitting with hundreds of private clients and teaching thousands of students, I'm convinced that the bulk of our fear, anxiety and stress originates in failing to understand our individuality. We are fundamentally unaware of our uniqueness, and therefore, quite terrified of exploring our fears of inadequacy.

Internal Vigilance

In 2013, I was asked to develop an eight-hour self-awareness and emotional intelligence training for the Orange County California Sheriff's Academy with funding from the Rancho Santiago Community College District. Our objective was to expand situational awareness to include greater self-awareness — an internal vigilance we described as ***Fearless Intelligence***.

By expanding my classroom training into this book, I'm able to incorporate fascinating and challenging concepts from education, psychology, ontology, philosophy and physics that go far beyond the immediate needs of a law enforcement academy.

Fearless Intelligence is a wisdom training in the tradition of the ancient Hermetic, Hellenic and Neo-Platonic Mystery Schools of Alexandria, as well as the mystical Yogic, Vedantic and Tantric philosophies of old Hindustan. While grounded in the metaphysical prehistory of the world, it's also a distinct application of three well-established, contemporary practices: *Mindfulness, Stress Reduction* and *Emotional Intelligence*. The golden thread linking these fields of study is self-awareness for its capacity to continually elevate consciousness, insight, understanding, compassion, gratitude, loving-kindness and wisdom.

The practice of mindful self-awareness originated in the ancient East, at least 2,500 years ago, as a Buddhist technique known as Insight Meditation or *Vipassana* (Pali language, meaning: *"to see things as they are, clearly and deeply"*). Some researchers claim vipassana originated with the Vedas more than 5,500 years ago. However, since Bronze Age scholars had access to only the most rudimentary proto-writing, many of the original practices were forgotten as institutionalized religion grew from the embryonic Vedic philosophies.

Whether Siddhartha Gautama (Buddha Shakyamuni) discovered or re-discovered the technique, a contemporary science of *mindfulness* has emerged in the West. As its benefits are confirmed by empirical research, mindful self-awareness is significantly influencing the training programs of universities, athletic teams and businesses, as well as various spiritual practices.

The need for stress reduction techniques first became clear in 1936 following the publication of research titled *General Adaptation Syndrome* by Hungarian physician Hans Selye. Dr. Selye identified numerous psychological disorders and physical diseases caused by long-term exposure to *fight-or-flight* hormones generated by lifestyles of excessive stimulus and continual change.

The phrase *Emotional Intelligence* (EQ) is attributable to Daniel Goleman, a Harvard psychologist and New York Times journalist who published the groundbreaking book, *Emotional Intelligence* in 1995. In Goleman's view, EQ includes self-awareness, accountability for your responses, empathy and relationship management. While influencing all nine of the aptitudes in Howard Gardner's model of multiple intelligences, emotional intelligence is most relevant to the two that Gardner labels *intrapersonal* and *interpersonal*. For our part, **Fearless Intelligence** is centered on the intrapersonal, principally self-awareness and emotional management.

The Basic Problem and Its Solution

Humanity is presently contending with a crisis unlike any other in our history. Gross materialism, consumerism and *"winner take all"* capitalism have been purposefully conflated with the ideals of liberty, democracy and free enterprise. The resulting injustice, corruption, self-indulgence and decadence cannot be sustained.

In this 21st Century, you'd be hard-pressed to find an industrialized society anywhere on Earth that isn't riddled with corruption. Insatiable greed, cruelty and sexploitation is commonplace in the corridors of power in Washington D.C., Wall Street and Hollywood.

Increasingly, our schools, hospitals and prisons have been privatized and transformed into fraudulent for-profit ventures. Government at all levels, multi-national corporations, financial institutions, mass media, even mega-churches and sporting events are now owned and operated by people dedicated to short-term profit and power at the expense of enduring character, ethics, morality, kindness, peace and justice for all.

In less than two centuries, reckless industrialization has poisoned much of the planet's ecosystem — a life support system that has flourished for over three billion years. Continual warfare diverts resources from social needs to a bloated, scandal-ridden military-industrial complex.

The root cause in each case is fear and the ignorance it breeds. And the only solution is fearlessness and the intelligence it fosters.

Wake-up and Stay Woke

Fear is the **Great Controller**. Advertisers, corporate bosses, politicians — even pastors and parents — use fear to extract desired behaviors from those with low self-awareness. Lately, mass confusion, chaos and fear have been weaponized at the highest levels. Routine irritation, frustration and dismay leave most people feeling powerless to do anything about institutional depravity and injustice.

Our most foolish and self-destructive behavior is motivated by fear; *but it is not the fear of danger.* The fundamental fear that preys upon us comes from failing to understand ourselves — neither as unique individuals nor as collaborators in the interdependence that evolution favors and human survival demands. We struggle with life because our need to release tension, reflexive behavior, obsessive thoughts and sullen, defensive attitudes is unconsciously opposed by our fear of everything we do not understand.

Though fear divides, love unites — not only emotional love, but Love as Awareness. We must refine our *you-or-me* world into a *you-**and**-me* world by expanding self-awareness. Expanded awareness *(higher consciousness)* provides a more complete, elevated view of concept and consequence, plus greater creative insight, accelerated learning and an evolving ethic devoted to the greater good of all concerned.

A paradigm shift of such magnitude requires us to awaken from our collective nightmare of helplessness and victimization. The information and techniques in **Fearless Intelligence** will help you to understand yourself better, become more empathic and learn to value cooperation over competition. Only steadfast efforts to become fully aware of our heartache and confusion can redeem the vicious cycle of fear and ignorance into harmony, unity, peace and understanding.

There is no need to rush through this book. Read it slowly and deliberately. Consume it in bite-sized pieces, mindfully digesting each portion before moving on. As your awareness expands, discuss key concepts with your family, friends and associates. Explain, but more importantly, listen.

I value your feedback.

*Whether you read this entire book or
only the chapters you find most relevant,
please post your sincere and honest review at:*

FearlessIntelligence.com/review

Thank you.

CHAPTER 1 — WHO AM I?

We are smarter than we think — intelligent in ways
our logical minds cannot comprehend.

During the summer between my junior and senior years at Michigan State University, I had a one-week vacation from my radio news job at WILS-AM & FM in Lansing. I had been planning a camping trip for months, carefully choosing which lakes I'd fish and the campgrounds where I'd pitch my tent each night.

As the date approached, I purchased or borrowed everything I'd need — sleeping bag, tent, camp stove, water jugs, large cooler, flashlights and assorted fishing gear. I even had a small aluminum jon boat that was light enough to hoist onto my car's roof rack without help.

Soon after my pre-dawn departure, a radiant sunny morning unfolded before me as I rolled into the dense pine woodlands of Northern Michigan. I lowered the car windows to enhance the fresh, resinous fragrances of the forest. The narrow, two-lane highway drew me deeper and deeper into the same timberlands my great-grandfather and his oxen, Pat and Mike, had logged after the Civil War. Hiking, camping and fishing across Michigan's Lower Peninsula was a big part of my heritage, and I felt fortunate to be speeding along in a car rather than walking or riding in an oxcart.

I was at least 25 or 30 miles from the nearest town when I heard a pop, then a hissing sound, followed by three or four loud engine knocks. Swerving to the shoulder of the road, I nervously raised the hood.

The top radiator hose hissed and spit at me like a hostile cobra. Annoyed at myself, my first thoughts were defensive. *"Everyone carries a spare tire, why don't we all carry spare radiator hoses, too,"* I demanded of myself.

I got no satisfaction from my instinctive efforts to avoid self-blame. Yet my ego persisted, insisting, *"Hey, this could've happened to anyone"* — a true, but irrelevant statement.

I was stranded and unable to recall when I had last seen another car along this secluded country lane. There were no phone boxes in the woods and no cell phones in those days.

The forest crowded in on me. Silence reigned but for a gentle breeze skimming across the tops of the tallest pines. Somehow, the sunny day seemed not so bright or cheery.

My legs felt slightly weak and wobbly, so I sat sideways in the front seat with my door open and my feet on the ground. My mind rushed through its own agenda.

"There's no one else out here," it warned. *"It could be hours before anyone drives by. This is serious. You may have to sleep in the car tonight."*

Only then did I remember there was a tent in my car, followed by an instantaneous revelation. Fireworks lit up the inside of my skull as I remembered why I was here — *to go camping!*

Everything I needed to survive was packed into my car. I could set up my tent beside the road, break out my camp stove, make hot coffee and cook a warm meal — anytime, anywhere. *What was I worried about?*

I was surprised to hear myself laugh out loud as I assured myself, *"This is not a problem."* The sun shone more brightly and the birds sang again as I realized I had arrived at the first campsite of my vacation.

Somewhat stunned by the revelation, I hadn't even begun to unpack when I heard the faint but distinctive sound of a car on the highway. Looking up and down the road, I squinted to find the car heading my way. As it came closer, I realized it was actually a truck. Wait, it was a tow truck.

I had turned 21 just six months earlier, but my real coming of age transpired on that rural Michigan highway. Only a small part of reality is done to us. Most of our experience is determined by how we perceive and respond to circumstances, events and relationships, especially when they appear to be beyond our control.

The 14th Century German mystic Johannes Tauler wrote, *"If I were a king and did not know it, I would not be a king."* Like my roadside dilemma, the core of our problems does not exist in the external world. Our difficulties live, primarily, as internal distortions generated, shaped and sustained by a lack of self-awareness. Anxiety, frustration and despair further degrade awareness and understanding.

Awareness (consciousness) is fundamental to existance — the Cause of All That Is. The individual mind is an allusion to self-awareness. It is more than the brain, because the body plays an integral role in everything the mind does. Both emotional and physical feelings are experienced throughout the body. Without Awareness, existence is meaningless, for nothing could be felt, seen or heard.

The question that took up residence within me that day was, *"How can I inhabit each moment, expanding my awareness of the perceptions that pass through my mind?"* While camping and fishing in the forests of Northern Michigan, I began to pursue the extraordinary wisdom of Awareness — the invisible essence of being.

In the half century since then, my quest has taken me through philosophy, comparative religion, mysticism, psychology, anthropology and countless personal development programs. In addition to various exercises at the end of each chapter, this book concludes with a series of practical tools and techniques you can practice for the rest of your life — skills for understanding, solving problems and living happily ever after.

Growing Up

I was four or five years old when my parents purchased their first television. Suddenly, graphic news of world events poured into our living room. The cruelty and injustice of war, racism and poverty became evident to me by my early teens.

As the first TV generation, baby-boomers were idealistic, but also smart enough to see the futility of trying to change the world through political reform alone. Many of us recognized the need to transform the views of the newsmakers and media commentators — or become them. By my 22nd birthday, I'd earned my bachelor's degree in broadcasting and journalism.

I also knew I needed to better understand myself before I could inform and influence others. My education had taught me many things about the world, but almost nothing about myself.

I replaced my naive desire for a problem-free life with an aspiration to become a better problem-solver. My subsequent search for a common thread running through my difficulties led directly to my fear and obliviousness. In time, I realized I was undiscovered, undeveloped and lacking self-awareness.

Finally free from schoolwork, I immersed myself in the fledgling *"human potential movement"* of the 1970s. As my awareness grew, my need to be right was replaced by a realization that *all* ideas, beliefs and opinions have relative degrees of merit. I learned the benefits of acknowledging other points of view, even when I strongly disagreed.

I also recognized the greatest of all fears is not death, pain or danger, but rather who we may be. Those with the courage to explore their individuality eventually recognize the glorious, incomparable uniqueness of every single thing. In a universe that refuses to replicate snowflakes, flowers or grains of sand, each one of us embodies diversity and harmony — an expanded Awareness called Peace and Love that redeems fear and ignorance.

The Counterculture's Search for Self-awareness

In the 1960s, the emotional sensitivity and heightened awareness resulting from the popular use of marijuana, LSD and other mind-expanding psychedelics led beatniks and Bohemian hippies to refer to themselves as *heads, freaks* and *flower children*. Informed by the lyrics of popular songs, alternative newspapers and counterculture books, baby-boomers began searching for each other to commiserate, organize against the War in Vietnam, and build support for civil rights, feminism and environmental protection. Gradually, the quest for higher consciousness, peace and love shifted from psychedelic drugs to mysticism.

The year 1967 was a significant turning point, often called the *Summer of Love*. In January of '67, no less than 25,000 people gathered in

San Francisco's Golden Gate Park for the first Human Be-In. The event was organized to rally opposition to a new California law banning the possession and use of LSD. Featured speakers included the High Priests of LSD, Dr. Timothy Leary and Dr. Richard Alpert; Beat poets Allen Ginsberg, Gary Snyder and Lawrence Ferlinghetti; plus live music by the Grateful Dead, Jefferson Airplane, Janis Joplin and Quicksilver Messenger Service.

Several months later, Firesign Theatre comedian Peter Bergman used his Radio Free Oz program on KPFK-FM to promote the first Love-in at Elysian Park in Los Angeles. Countless Love-ins followed from coast-to-coast offering one-day sanctuaries for psychedelic rock music, dancing, meditation and copious drug use.

Intending to elevate rock 'n' roll and blues from a trendy fad to an established musical genre, an unprecedented three-day Pop Music Festival was held in June of '67 at the site of the annual Monterey Jazz Festival. By later that summer, an estimated 100,000 flower children had spontaneously migrated to San Francisco's Haight-Ashbury neighborhood to participate in the counter-culture's *Summer of Love*.

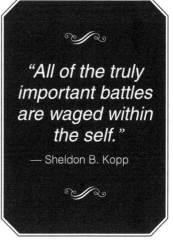

"All of the truly important battles are waged within the self."

— Sheldon B. Kopp

Soon after the June release of *Sgt. Pepper's Lonely Hearts Club Band*, the Beatles announced their affiliation with the Indian guru, Maharishi Mahesh Yogi, founder of Transcendental Meditation (TM). The eminent Harvard psychologist and LSD researcher Dr. Richard Alpert traveled to India seeking enlightenment and returned as a guru named Baba Ram Dass. Also in 1967, Dr. Martin Luther King Jr. nominated a Vietnamese Zen Buddhist monk, Thich Nhat Hanh, for the Nobel Peace Prize, and His Holiness the Dalai Lama made his first trip abroad since his exile from Tibet to India in 1959.

My fascination with mysticism, altered states, meditation and self-hypnosis began in the early 1960s when I saw a stage hypnotist induce trance states on the TV variety show, *Art Linkletter's House Party*. As a young teen, I ordered my first book about hypnosis with a coupon clipped from the back of a comic book.

My college experiences with LSD revealed the vibrancy and vitality of Divinity in everything everywhere. I clearly experienced myself as part of a universal collective, but the orthodox monotheistic view of God as an invisible hominid living far above the clouds now seemed nonsensical. Instead, the psychedelic consensus that *"Love is everywhere"* made the monism of Eastern philosophy reasonable and appealing to much of my generation. Soon, an interest in meditation and mindfulness was flourishing among baby-boomers.

I was also impressed in my college years with the biography of trance medium Edgar Cayce, *There Is a River* by Thomas Sugrue. During the early '70s, I read *Seth Speaks,* a trance-channeled manuscript by Jane Roberts, *Self-Hypnotism* by Leslie LeCron, and the classics, *As a Man Thinketh* by James Allen, *The Varieties of Religious Experience* by William James and *The Science of Mind* by Ernest Holmes. In 1974, a 40-hour self-hypnosis training called Silva Mind Control provided me with a variety of practical tools for improved concentration, stress reduction, memory, problem solving, pain management and accelerated healing.

By 1981, I was teaching meditation, guided imagery and self-hypnosis at *Live and Learn*, a nonprofit personal development center in Sherman Oaks, California, run by accelerated learning pioneer, Steven Snyder. My workshops were called *Integrated Thinking,* though we were actually teaching students to blend and balance an enhanced emotional awareness with their logical and intuitive thoughts.

The workshop was expanded in 1984 and renamed *Integrated Living* — a 12-hour seminar offered at both the Los Angeles and Long Beach Convention centers. Our slogan was, *"Check it out. Feel it out. Act it out"* — inspired by Napoleon Hill's renowned triplet, *"If you can conceive it and believe it, you can achieve it."*

Working as a radio journalist and talk show host at ABC Radio in Los Angeles, I was confident and successful, but still somehow incomplete. As I approached my mid-30s, I began to realize how the urge to know myself better was more emotional than mental. I knew how to *think* about my emotions, but I had no idea how to understand their significance.

I met Joel Isaacs, a Santa Monica-based Reichian therapist at a *Live and Learn* seminar. Joel was non-threatening, knowledgeable and experienced, so

22

I scheduled an intake session hoping he could aid my shift from mostly cerebral to an expanded emotional awareness.

In our second meeting, Joel asked, *"Are you willing to walk on the edge of your feelings?"* I wasn't sure what he meant, but I was eager to try anything that would help me sort things out. In my brain, Mick Jagger's petulant lyric, *"I can't get no satisfaction; 'cause I try, and I try, and I try and I try,"* played over and over, like the soundtrack of my life.

During our next few sessions, I began to feel the full range of emotions in my body and understand them intuitively. I was amazed to find expanded awareness, intelligence and insight hidden inside my emotional hurt and heartache. Of course, I'd always known that big, overwhelming emotions — anger, sadness and excitement, too — affected me physically; and emotions were called feelings after all. Slowly it dawned on me just how similar the intimations of my emotions were to my physical feelings. Like physical pain, heartache and confusion are symptoms that need awareness and understanding, not repression.

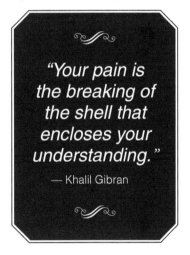

"Your pain is the breaking of the shell that encloses your understanding."

— Khalil Gibran

Early on, Joel and I found deeply buried despair — the kind of fear and alienation that children suffer. More than once in our sessions, I wept uncontrollably. Never before had I allowed myself to release such all-consuming anguish.

Oddly, Joel had to teach me *how* to cry. He insisted I breathe deeply, look directly into his eyes and let go.

The dam broke. Tears drained my reservoir of accumulated misery. I sobbed like an infant, without reservation. Clearly, something was leaving my body. The relief was palpable.

I was deeply moved one day when Joel hugged me during a crying jag — blown-away by how safe it made me feel. I realized I had no memory of my father ever embracing me when I cried or was frightened. Instead, he would

23

amplify my heartache and fear with threats and shouts of, *"Shut up. Shut up. Stop crying now, or I'll give you something to cry about!"*

Yes, this was very different. At one point, an explosion of self-awareness shook me into realizing I really had been a good kid. I was *not* a bad little boy, much less *rotten*, as I'd been told repeatedly. It was as if a 12-year-old inside of me suddenly burst out of a prison, shouting, *"I didn't do anything wrong. It wasn't my fault. I'm not bad."* In that instant, I had forgiven myself.

Releasing my old, pent-up fear and desolation soon allowed me to feel new peak levels of happiness and contentment — often for no apparent reason. The psychological stress and physical tension I'd carried was no longer inhibiting my inborn joy and love. The spontaneous, unbounded delight seen in very young children began to flow through me. I felt warm, vibrant and complete.

I realized the experience of being alive had more to do with emotional feelings than mental thoughts. It was a wonderful and joyous insight.

Taking It to the Streets

The romantic poet Lord Byron wrote, *"All who joy would win must share it. Happiness was born a Twin."* In that sense, I felt compelled to use my career as a radio talk show host to broadcast my thrilling news. Without psychoanalysis, without a need to comprehend my parents' behavior, without slicing and dicing my childhood and adolescence into tiny pieces, I was free. With Joel's guidance and belief in our innate human wisdom, I discovered the keys to my self-imposed prison of fear and ignorance.

It was the early 1980s and my radio talk shows were broadcast across Southern California on KABC-AM and KLOS-FM, sister stations owned and operated by the American Broadcasting Company (ABC, Inc.). A Hollywood cowboy and ex-governor of California, Ronald Reagan had just moved into the White House, and his daughter Maureen and son Michael were soon hosting talk radio programs on KABC-AM. Secret Service men-in-black roamed the hallways whenever the Reagan kids celebrated their father's party line over the airwaves.

A new uber-conservatism was flourishing. Big government and big unions were the problem. And somehow, big corporations were the solution. Trickle-down *voodoo economics* turned reality upside-down. Fast and loose talk of winning a nuclear war with highly accurate *first-strike* ICBMs and an anti-ballistic missile system dubbed *Star Wars* had angered the Soviets, terrified our European allies and numbed America's silent majority into a mass stupor.

TV and radio talk shows quickly degenerated into echo chambers affirming only what the conservative hosts and their cherry-picked guests proffered. Meaningful discussions were abolished as nuance was replaced by all-or-nothing rhetoric. Like other industries, the consolidation of ownership continued so that, as of this book's publication in 2018, only six corporations own more than 90% of all outlets. And print media — newspapers, magazines and book publishers — are struggling to avoid extinction. In the last decade, leisure time spent reading has fallen by 22%.[1]

Targeting a Demand

I saw a need for diversity and a demand for a more comprehensive discussion of current events and issues. Referring to my talk show as *Open Conversation*, I targeted *why* my radio guests and callers held this or that belief. Although I worked at ABC Radio's two flagship stations in L.A. for over a decade, callers were repeatedly caught off-guard by questions about *why* they thought, felt or behaved as they did. Everyone has opinions, but few people understand why.

> *"Perhaps everything that frightens us is, in its deepest essence, something helpless that wants our love."*
>
> — Rainer Maria Rilke

It was fascinating. Listeners loved the sudden exposure of emotionally naked callers, casting about and awkwardly stammering to explain the feelings, beliefs, attitudes and motives behind their rigid opinions. For the most part, I was sympathetic and supportive, pointing out the benefits of becoming more self-aware through relaxation, contemplation and meditation. But it was a *show,* so I didn't hesitate to eviscerate bigots, reactionaries and simply nasty or hostile callers — anyone who promoted fear and ignorance to my audience.

As popular as my program became, corporate executives never understood how to sell it to advertisers. Yet it created a demand for me as a public speaker and seminar leader. By the late '80s, I'd replaced my career as a broadcast journalist and talk show host with personal development services — private training, counseling and coaching from an educational rather than a psycho-therapeutic viewpoint. My emphasis centered on the use of guided imagery in deeply relaxed alpha brainwave states to develop concentration, emotional intelligence, critical thinking and peak performance skills. With experience and maturity, I discovered the benefits of vipassana (mindfulness meditation) for developing self-awareness and self-realization.

"If you're going through hell, keep going."
— Winston Churchill

"The best way out is always through."
— Robert Frost

Exercises:

To practice visualizing with your mind's eye, sit down and close your eyes. Inhale slowly and deeply, and as you exhale, just as slowly, begin to relax your entire body. As you allow your breathing to find its own rhythm, create and sense a letting go feeling in your body from head to toe.

With your eyes still closed, imagine a small movie screen floating in front of your forehead. Imagine, projected on that screen, the image of a stop sign. It's red with four white letters — S-T-O-P. What else do you notice about the stop sign? How many sides does it have?

In your mind's eye, change that traffic sign to one that's yellow and says Y-I-E-L-D. What color are the letters? What is the shape of the sign? Imagine walking around to the backside of the sign. What color is the back? Can you see how is the sign attached to the pole?

Visualize the letters of the alphabet, one at a time? Are they capital letters or lower case? As you move through the alphabet, imagine each letter disappearing in a different way. One vanishes in a puff of smoke. Another quickly melts, collapsing into a puddle. The next letter goes up in flames, and so on.

CHAPTER 2 —
WHAT IS AWARENESS?

Everyone is born with some degree of innate intelligence.
Knowledge must be taught and experienced.
Wisdom is a product of self-awareness.

Wisdom is the supreme intelligence — the awareness of being aware that overshadows all feeling, experience, thought, knowledge and behavior. As ***Fearless Intelligence***, wisdom is also the exalted Awareness of Love as the essential Life Force (prana, chi, mana, orenda).

In this age of expanding computer intelligence and robotics, machines will get better at thinking and learning, but without self-awareness, they will never be wise. Smartphones and other high-tech gadgets process information and store knowledge, but cannot understand why. They are incapable of discerning the motives behind their programs and cannot imagine intuitive insight, a conscience, emotional feelings, empathy or compassion — vital qualities of conscious, self-aware beings.

The grand secrets of existence are not restricted to the mountaintop, the sky or some remote corner of the Cosmos. The wisdom of awareness is everywhere, illuminating and animating All Things — as above, so below; around us, within us, closer than our own breath. Without awareness, nothing exists.

We cannot reason our way to wisdom. As Awareness, wisdom is intuitive and comprehensive. The erudite virtues of wisdom are more dependent upon self-awareness than knowledge of the world.

Fortunately, wisdom can be cultivated by a fearless will to explore everything we do not understand about our self. To be most effective, we must practice this contemplation in quiet, tranquil states, devoid of tension, anxiety, confusion, overthinking and emotional drama.

Our understanding of self as a universal, yet unique being influences everything we know. We are One Awareness, eternal and infinite, exploring individuality in time and space. Those who do not understand themselves as inimitable individuals tend to be anxious, self-centered, defensive and insecure. Rather than recognize their emotional feelings as personal responses, they view themselves as victims and blame others for the way they feel.

How Do You Feel?

The subjectivity of self is revealed by our emotional feelings, for mental thoughts are principally objective and dispassionate. Understanding our self and our connection to all other life forms requires high levels of self-awareness and emotional intelligence.

Do not ignore, deny or resist emotions that hurt or frighten you. Embrace them and plumb their depths. As you discover the gift of wisdom they represent, you will also become free of fear and heartache. This is *Fearless Intelligence* — the path of wisdom.

Typically, we are much less aware of our emotions than our thoughts. Unconscious fear and heartache can hijack intention and drive behavior without the moderation of reasoning. By developing self-awareness, we can observe, identify and understand the subtlest feelings with equanimity.

Escalating stimulus often confuses and frightens us, which promotes frantic thoughts, hysterical feelings and impulsive behavior. Expanded self-awareness allows us to witness and regulate our thoughts and feelings, letting us affirm those we regard as appropriate while rejecting those we do not. As a result, we are better able to replace reflexive reactions with deliberate initiatives.

If all insects were to disappear from Earth, the ecosystem would collapse, and every other living creature would soon die. However, if humans disappeared, the ecosystem would flourish — suggesting we are not only unnecessary but an existential threat.

Human corruption is caused by a single misperception. We believe each of us is a detached, isolated and autonomous being. Insects cooperate, while humans compete. The growth of self-awareness leads to the enlightened recognition that we are *not* the separated ego-self. The true self is an integrated subdivision of a single, cohesive Life, expressing in multiple, diverse forms.

Ultimately, the extraordinary wisdom of Awareness replaces the struggles and miseries of living with a clear understanding that we are components of One Life. Despite appearances, we are not separate from anything. We are interdependent fragments of a single Universe. We may see ourselves as differentiated droplets, but in fact, we are the ocean. There's only One of us here, and truly, nothing to fear.

The Components of Wisdom

Psychologists working with the Max Planck Institutes developed a model of wisdom in the late 1980s, which they summarized as *"expertise in the fundamental pragmatics of life."* Known as the **Berlin Wisdom Project**, their study identified five basic qualities of wisdom:

1. ***Rich factual knowledge*** of human nature and the physical universe in which we live,

2. ***Rich procedural knowledge*** about human judgment in problem-solving and decision-making,

3. ***Lifespan contextualism***, which refers to the ability to see life's big pictures, how their relationships change and interact,

4. ***Relativism***, which is a recognition of the merits of varying values, goals and priorities, and …

5. ***Uncertainty***, meaning the awareness and anticipation of what remains unknown.

Since then, other writers on the subject have suggested additional wisdom traits, including emotional management, humility, empathy, compassion, honesty and authenticity. For our purposes, ***Fearless Intelligence*** views wisdom as five types of awareness:

1. ***Consciousness*** — awareness of the perceptions that pass through the mind; the elevated point-of-view provided by observing how

our thoughts and feelings lead to particular behaviors, relationships, circumstances and events.

2. *Intuition* — awareness of spontaneous insights and comprehension of transpersonal, spiritual intelligence.

3. *Conscience* — awareness of the values, ethics and motives that stand above mental intelligence.

4. *Synergy* — awareness of the interdependence, harmony and unity of all things in the human, animal, plant and mineral kingdoms.

5. *Mysteries* — awareness of what is *not* known and which may never be understood. Western philosophers call this *philosophical humility* or *Socratic ignorance.* In Buddhist philosophy, it's found in the aspiration to develop *Beginner's mind,* sometimes called *Don't-know mind.* There is always more to be understood than we can imagine.

Fearless Intelligence is a calm, peaceful and still level of equanimity. It features the realization that we can redeem all fear and ignorance with elevated self-awareness, for Awareness (Love) is the ultimate Reality.

While people may have their own sense of the meaning of life, our common purpose is to evolve — not to merely adapt, but to grow, improve and advance, unfolding our most Divine qualities. We naturally become wiser and more loving over time. Yet we can accelerate the expansion of that self-awareness by persistently replacing fear and ignorance with love and understanding. And by helping others do the same, we conspire with the Universal Longing to realize our ultimate potential.

Fearlessness is not a destination or level of attainment, but rather a progressive unfoldment of Loving Awareness. Ironically, fear has an essential role to play when not repressed, ignored or denied. Even the tiniest bit of anxiety or heartache signals an opportunity to learn about our uniqueness and personal role in the Grand Intention of the Cosmos.

Fear Degrades Self-awareness

Compared to the rest of the world, most Americans enjoy great material prosperity, yet they remain unfulfilled. The Internet connects us to the world, yet our alienation and loneliness persist. We have access to more information than we can imagine but know little about ourselves. We're awake, but unaware because our greatest fear is uncovering who we may be. Just as the wheel and electricity existed before they were discovered, self-awareness is the *Essence of Being,* though few people have yet to realize it.

As both a cause and a result of ignorance, fear pulls at our hearts and minds. It is the brain's appeal for more information, and thus uncovers opportunities to develop peace, love and wisdom.

It's a mistake to portray human fear with animal references like chicken, scaredy-cat, sheepish, timid as a mouse, spineless as a jellyfish, deer in the headlights, playing possum or burying your head in the sand like an ostrich. No creature in the animal kingdom, feral or domesticated, becomes frightened as easily as humans.

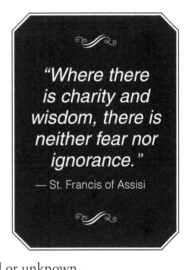

"Where there is charity and wisdom, there is neither fear nor ignorance."

— St. Francis of Assisi

Like other animals, humans fear the mere appearance of danger — real or imagined. However, the human tendency to ruminate upon thoughts and feelings promotes exaggerated fears of everything misunderstood or unknown.

Everyone is afraid at different times, to varying degrees and often for no discernable reason, because *all fear is fear of the unknown.* Fear does *not* signal danger. It has evolved to alert us to confusion, ignorance and unawareness, whether dangerous or not.

The negative thoughts and hurtful feelings fostered by fear, anxiety and stress are edifying symptoms of whatever we do not understand. It's wise to reflect upon them, as well as on any inherent unwillingness to face the whole truth when it makes us uncomfortable.

Emotions are intoxicating and contagious. Besides damaging physical health, heightened emotions can stress and impair mental and emotional intelligence and judgment. Fear and anxiety befuddle us to a point where we fail to realize how obtuse, insensitive and unaware we've become.

Self-awareness and intelligence are reduced whenever we ignore, deny or defend fear. Carried as muscular tension, unresolved fear instigates vicious cycles of even more anxiety, stress and fear. The cyclonic nature of fear and confusion, each feeding the other, is often mistaken for stupidity. But the root problem is a lack of self-awareness, not an absence of intellect.

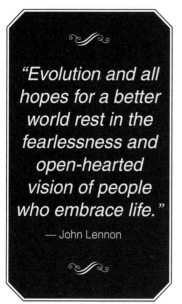

"Evolution and all hopes for a better world rest in the fearlessness and open-hearted vision of people who embrace life."

— John Lennon

Relaxation and stress reduction break the cycle. When the physical body feels relaxed and safe, brainwave frequencies lower, which provides focused, calm insight into whatever our heartache and confusion are trying to reveal. *Fear and tension reduce intelligence. Feeling safe and relaxed expands intelligence.*

Without a doubt, the best way to enhance self-awareness and intelligence-on-demand is to physically release the tension precipitated by fear. That's **Fearless Intelligence** — a skill set for greatly expanded self-awareness and intelligence.

Unfortunately, poor self-awareness leads most people to misjudge themselves as somehow inferior and inadequate. As we recognize the growth steps and stages our fears offer, we gain the self-realization of our genuine authenticity and uniqueness with humility, grace and gratitude.

We should never be ashamed of our fear regardless of its name — heartache, anxiety, stress, tension, pressure, panic, terror, horror, phobias, worry, doubt, dread, trepidation, consternation, nervous apprehension or concern. Fright is a vital signal that alerts us to a need for better understanding.

Fear Supports All Heartache and Upset

Fear is much more than a single emotion. It is the common link in all hurtful feelings, physical and emotional. Intense fear inflames anger, hate, envy, contempt, disgust, sadness and confusion. Over prolonged periods, fear also fosters an inability to feel much of anything, even fear itself. This dazed and confused state, known clinically as *psychic numbing*, is brought on by the fear rising out of severe trauma, grief or chronic depression.

Attempts to overcome or defeat fear are misguided. Since fear manifests as physical tension, attempts to conquer it only generate more tension. Instead, fear must be released. Complaints about *"feeling stuck"* are born of a victim's innate *"holding on"* reflex to fear and psychic numbing — holding on to physical tension, emotional distress and mental confusion. Humans increase their fear when they try to overwhelm tension rather than let it go.

Many people sleepwalk along a nightmarish treadmill, terrified to awaken to even greater fear and confusion. Ironically, it's only by facing our fear that enhanced self-awareness can reveal the joy and vision of a meaningful, fulfilling and fearless life.

> "When we get too caught up in the busyness of the world, we lose connection with one another and ourselves."
>
> — Jack Kornfield

Love Is Awareness

Fear and confusion signal the absence of self-awareness. Love and understanding indicate the presence of self-awareness. So once identified, fear can be recognized as the brain's request for greater insight and understanding.

Fear is a survival-based alert that tells us to relax and explore the empty caverns in our self-awareness. Because there's little others can teach us about our individuality, self-discovery is, ultimately, a solo journey. Why do we think, feel and act in the ways we do? What do we care about, and why?

You can't *"dance to your own tune"* if you refuse to hear the music. A similar allegory suggests most people die with *"their task unfinished and their song unsung."* [2] With few exceptions, we are oblivious to our eccentricities — uninformed, misinformed, confused or in denial about who we are beyond the characters and roles we play to gain the acceptance of others.

Physicist Albert Einstein is best known for having integrated matter and energy, space and time, gravity and electromagnetism into One Thing. However, his Special Theory of Relativity equating matter and energy ($E=mc^2$) fails to address one other meaningful phenomenon — substantial portions of the material world are conscious. Though comprised of the same chemical elements as inanimate, inorganic matter, life in endless diversity is self-aware.

"Expose yourself to your deepest fear; after that, fear has no power, and the fear of freedom shrinks and vanishes. You are free."

— Jim Morrison

Most well-educated people realize that all living beings are made from the same chemicals and compounds as the earth's molten core and rock-strewn mantle. Yet rarely do we turn that awareness around and ask, *"Why do some of these chemicals and minerals organize themselves into sentient life forms? What is the self-awareness that inhabits this body of rocky soil and water? How does this stardust become aware of itself as microbes, plants, animals and people?"*

The majority of empirical scientists in the 21st Century still favors the 200-year-old view attributed to the University of Berlin's Helmholtz school. Rejecting vitalism and other metaphysical and spiritual views of animation, German scientists committed themselves to the hypothesis that physiochemical forces govern living organisms. This idea downgrades consciousness and awareness to a mere epiphenomenon — a secondary by-product or effect of the physical brain rather than a self-determining cause of neurological stimulation.

As early as the Fourth Century BCE, Aristotle's metaphysics suggested that the physical world is a projection of the observer's self-awareness or level of consciousness. The assumption that conscious awareness must be a function of brain chemistry is comparable to a person who has never seen a radio or cell phone assuming the sounds are coming *from* the device rather than *through* it.

Swiss psychiatrist Carl G. Jung's concept of a collective unconscious bolsters the emerging spiritual ecology movement. Together they postulate a comprehensive inter-reliance of mental awareness, spiritual archetypes and physical forms as sacred emanations of a holistic, holographic Universe.

Human burial sites and other shrines dating back as far as 130,000 years ago show a loving, spiritual connection between members of family, tribe, animals and the realms of Nature. In much of the world, this love is attributed to one or more Divine Beings living far away. However, throughout Asia, the earliest known belief systems are non-dual, implying a Divine Awareness containing All That Is.

The dualistic view of a transcendent Creator living outside Its creation evolved into Abrahamic monotheism — Judeo-Christianity and Islam. A non-dual view of the Universe as One Thing developed into monistic and non-theistic philosophies, predominantly Hinduism, Buddhism, Taoism and Sikhism.

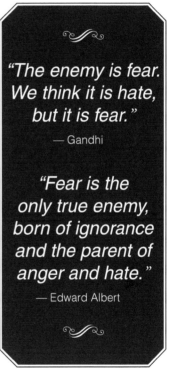

"The enemy is fear. We think it is hate, but it is fear."
— Gandhi

"Fear is the only true enemy, born of ignorance and the parent of anger and hate."
— Edward Albert

The Ground of Being

Awareness is the Absolute Ground of Being. It is autonomous and superior to knowledge, for all thought, feeling, behavior and perception rely on self-awareness. Conscious awareness distinguishes the enduring Self from our transient thoughts and feelings.

For the most part, we remain unaware of awareness itself. Self-awareness has an ebb and flow, meaning our potential for self-realization varies from moment to moment. We lose much of the splendor and joy of being alive when we analyze our heartache and confusion. To be *aware of being aware* (metacognition, meta-awareness), we must knowingly focus our attention on the fullness of the present moment without judgment.

Unmanaged heartache and confusion diminish awareness, suppressing our understanding of self and the world. Stress reduction not only expands awareness of emotional feelings, it also promotes an awareness of what we do *not* know or understand.

In other words, a willingness to understand hurtful feelings and the fear that provokes them are essential to recovery. Even when we're confused about what we do not know about our self, there is wisdom in accepting that our search will never end. There will always be fresh perspectives and redemptive awareness awaiting discovery. The awareness that there is always more to learn leads us to greater self-discovery, happiness, peace-of-mind and fulfillment.

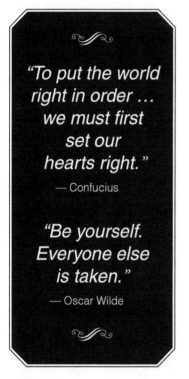

"To put the world right in order ... we must first set our hearts right."
— Confucius

"Be yourself. Everyone else is taken."
— Oscar Wilde

Comedian Lily Tomlin has quipped, *"If love is the answer, could you please repeat the question?"* Once we appreciate Love as the expanded awareness that emerges in the absence of fear (Fearless Intelligence), our response could be, *"Love answers all questions."*

Christ's allusion to *"Love your enemies"* expresses Love as much more than emotional affinity. Love is the awareness, insight and understanding that empower us to recognize fear as ignorance, especially about our unique self. Danger may appear outside of us, but our fear lives within. Our primary enemy is the fear of our own egoic shadow. We must slay our inner demons to protect ourselves from the ill will of others and the perils of circumstance.

How can we attain this Higher Ground? Awareness is cultivated through stress reduction and mindfulness. This book, **Fearless Intelligence**, offers several simple techniques to target the roots of our fear.

Many of us assume heartache and anger generate fear, but the reverse is even more to the point. As unawareness, fear spawns and nourishes all heartache, hatred, greed, violence and cruelty. We are trapped between the fear of understanding ourselves and the fear of *not* understanding ourselves — between the fear of success and the fear of failure.

Multiple Intelligences

Observing our spontaneous thought processes teaches us that, day and night, the mind thinks according to its own agenda. Thinking is what it does. It cannot be stopped or paused for more than a moment or two.

We also learn that all thought distorts our perception of reality. We see separation, though everything is connected. We see solid and liquid forms where only energy swirls and dances. We experience conflict where harmony rules the day. We suffer anxiety and confusion despite a reality that is peaceful and resolved. We can transcend our thoughts by learning to identify, instead, with Awareness — the Love which is true, infinite and eternal.

Logical, rational analysis and even creative thought is but a sketch — a series of lines drawn around and through our lives. Our emotions provide the light, color, warmth, fragrance, music and drama. Though we welcome our positive, love-based feelings, most of us resist feeling fear and discontent. Yet without the full range of emotions, life would be barren and meaningless. Every bit of resistance to feeling *any* emotion reduces our awareness of all other feelings; and over the long-term, our heartache and confusion intensify.

"Love is fearless in the midst of the sea of fear."
— Rumi

Expanded awareness (higher consciousness) requires us to face and embrace our emotional angst. Only by fully feeling our distress and despair will the insight and understanding that results release us from our heartache and confusion.

Emotional intelligence (EQ) is the portal to an expanded awareness of who we are and what we're capable of accomplishing. By developing emotional intelligence, we gain clarity about who we are, based largely on what we want and why we care. Individuality is less about what we *think* of our self, than our awareness of how we *feel* emotionally. Ultimately, we must grow from *being aware* to *Being Awareness*.

The enhanced self-esteem and self-love produced by expanded awareness is neither egocentric nor selfish. True personal development exposes qualities of self that are humble and considerate. Increasing self-awareness reveals the mutual benefits of acting with civility, kindness, compassion and generosity.

Human evolution has not peaked. It is speeding up — not only our mental and physical prowess but also our emotional capacity for love, intuition, insight and understanding.[3]

In 1983, Harvard psychologist Dr. Howard Gardner challenged the traditional concept of intelligence as a single, unified aptitude. In his book, *Frames of Mind: The Theory of Multiple Intelligences*[4] and subsequent publications, Gardner proposed nine types of human intelligence:

1. ***Musical-rhythmic and harmonic*** — sensitivity to musical sounds: melody, harmony and rhythmic patterns.

2. ***Visual-spatial*** — inherently skilled in imagination, visualization and picturing with the mind's eye.

3. ***Verbal-linguistic*** — particularly gifted in language and word use; storytelling, reading and writing.

4. ***Logical-mathematical*** — the natural ability to conceptualize numbers, analytical reasoning and critical thinking.

5. ***Bodily-kinesthetic*** — muscle coordination, grace, balance and timing.

6. ***Naturalistic*** — those who are predominantly aware of their connection to the animal, plant and mineral kingdoms of Nature and their inter-reliance.

7. ***Existential*** — a transpersonal, metaphysical and spiritual awareness.

8. ***Intrapersonal*** — high self-awareness of one's strengths and weaknesses and the meaning of emotional feelings, moods, attitudes and motivations.

9. ***Interpersonal*** — naturally empathetic, skilled communicator and leader. Emotional intelligence is primarily a factor in the intrapersonal and

interpersonal. The emphasis of *Fearless Intelligence* is intrapersonal —
self-awareness and emotional management.

Neuroplasticity

The emerging field of neuroplasticity studies the way nerve pathways and
synapses in our brains respond to changes in environment, behavior, thoughts
and emotional feelings. Neuroscience has confirmed that in relaxed, mindful
states of expanded awareness, the adult human brain literally grows and adapts
to the demands placed upon it — somewhat like a muscle.

Repeatedly, empirical research points to self-awareness as the key to
brain plasticity and our potential to accelerate the evolution of human
consciousness. Conversely, increasing levels of fear, anxiety and stress impede brain growth and neuroplasticity by limiting self-awareness to little
more than a survival-based binary absolutism — friend or foe, true or false,
all or nothing.

With the principles and tools presented in *Fearless Intelligence*, you can
radically improve your life in numerous ways:

- Literally grow a bigger, faster, smarter brain.

- Realize who you are, based upon what you truly care about and why.

- Identify the deepest motives behind your thoughts, feelings, speech
  and behavior.

- Find heartfelt meaning and purpose in your relationships, career,
  avocations and public service.

- Discover your unique inborn talents and skills.

- End the struggle of contriving and defending your false self and the
  englamoured roles you play.

- Step off the hamster wheel of material acquisition and status climbing.

- Accelerate your evolution, unfolding your ultimate destiny.

- Chart and navigate the wondrous adventure of living your dreams and goals.

- Become joyful, compassionate, fulfilled, free and happy for no reason.

- Cherish each moment by accepting the reality of material impermanence and eternal Love.

- Celebrate the ultimate supremacy of Love as Awareness that heals and redeems.

The Hidden Value of Fear

Many of my clients, students, radio listeners and friends have urged me to write books about my views on personal and spiritual development, but most have cautioned me to avoid discussing fear. They felt that most people are too frightened to face their fear. Yet one of my motives is to distinguish the appearance of danger from the more fundamental fear of confusion, ignorance and unawareness.

My primary intention is to assist my readers in their efforts to awaken. Mass media — entertainment, news, political, advertising and social platforms — share pervasive, computer-based behavior modification strategies. Algorithmic loops identify and exaggerate like-minded consumers, who then discover and network with each other.

Because fear, frustration and anger are more engaging than peace, love and understanding, a reactionary backlash will resist social progress. These spiraling loops of cultural partisanship fuel the divisiveness and hostility that has become so obvious.

The designers of this monetized engagement openly admit they are Directors of Programming, and we eagerly download and install their pernicious drivel into our neural wetware. Gross consumerism has already turned most of the people we know into sleepwalkers — those who do not read, question or think for themselves, much less choose their values or understand why they believe what they believe. From time to time, the best among us fall prey to this mindless entrainment.

In the long run, the dark side is not stronger than the light, but inclusivity and loving-kindness require the wisdom of awareness. Reading the following pages is the red pill that exposes the Matrix and leads to the liberating sagacity of self-realization.

The title of this book is **Fearless Intelligence**, so let's be clear at the outset. No one has ever lived a life without fear. Even enlightened spiritual masters like Christ and Buddha admit to having been afraid. The secret is to know ourselves well enough to believe in our innate wisdom and potential.

When we face fear, replace tension with relaxation and trust our intuition, profound insight, understanding and true wisdom will replace fear and the heartache it breeds. Awareness reveals and heals, replacing ignorance with understanding and repression with expression.

The secret to the redemptive, healing power of Love is Awareness. We use the word *love* as if it were an emotion, but it is not an emotion. Love is Awareness, Truth and Wisdom.

Love allows the One Life to express multiplicity without depletion. Expose your pain and confusion to expanded Awareness, for as you reveal it, and feel it, you heal it.

Exercise:

Reflect for just a few minutes on the central concepts presented in this chapter.

1. All fear is *"fear of the unknown"* — not a warning of imminent danger, but an indication of something that's not understood, whether dangerous or not. The most frightening unknown is not death, pain or danger, but who we may be as a truly unique individual.

2. Fear is the common stimulus behind the full range of hurtful emotions that alert us to ignorance, confusion or unawareness.

3. Individuality is less about *what we think* of our self than our awareness of *how we feel* emotionally. Conscious awareness is the understanding that distinguishes the enduring Self from our transient thoughts.

4. Unmanaged heartache and anxiety diminish awareness, suppressing our understanding of self and the world around us. Stress reduction expands awareness and emotional intelligence, revealing the meaning and significance of our distress.

*"We must face our fears without flinching.
We must honestly ask ourselves why we are afraid.
The confrontation will, to some measure, grant us power. We can never cure fear by the method of escapism. Nor can it be cured by repression.
The more we attempt to ignore and repress our fears, the more we multiply our inner conflicts and cause the mind to deteriorate into a slum district."*

— Dr. Martin Luther King Jr.

CHAPTER 3 —
WHAT IS FEAR?

*Fear is difficult to understand because
it's an effect of not understanding.*

I knew solo backpacking was a bad idea. Every hiking book I'd ever read cautioned against it. But my radio news jobs usually fell on weekends and I had trouble finding anyone to hike with me during the week. So I did a lot of day hiking and backpacking alone. Often I'd meet other solo hikers on the trail and, in time, I gave up my apprehension about it.

I was not a cross-country kind of guy. When I hiked my favorite trails — through California's Sierra Nevada Range, the Ventana Wilderness hot springs and crests overlooking Big Sur, the high desert in Joshua Tree National Park, Oregon's Three Sisters Wilderness, Maui's Haleakala Crater and Iao Valley or the Santa Monica Mountains Conservancy, San Gabriel Mountains and Angeles National Forest just above L.A. — I rarely stepped off the well-worn trails.

My most ambitious hike turned out to be the most perilous, and it's likely my troubles never would have occurred if I hadn't been hiking alone. I set out on a 50-mile ramble through the magnificent Sierra Nevada range — from Lodgepole (6,750 feet) in the giant Sequoia redwood forest, over Silliman Pass (10,200 feet), down through Sugarloaf Valley (7,000 feet), then up Deadman Canyon to Elizabeth Pass (11,370 feet) and back to Lodgepole through Bearpaw Meadow.

Well-conditioned backpackers can hike this loop in three or four days, but I allowed myself a full week. The best part of hiking alone is the freedom to straggle whenever you feel like it — to stop and read a book during the mid-afternoon heat, fish a stream or glacial lake — or even sleep-in a bit. And that's exactly what I did.

The toughest day was the climb from upper Ranger Meadow (9,800 feet) in Deadman Canyon over Elizabeth Pass (11,370 feet), then descending 3,350 feet to Lone Pine Creek. Though it was mid-August, I encountered a strange mix of misty rain, snow, hail and lightning as I surmounted the narrow gap.

From Elizabeth Pass, the views of Valhalla, the Triple Divide and the peaks of the Great Western Divide are spectacular. Silence reigned but for the wind spilling over the ragged summits. Slowly turning, I was spellbound by the ineffable beauty of the *Range of Light* — a term coined only 100 years earlier by explorer John Muir as he wrote, *"After ten years spent in the heart of it, rejoicing and wondering, bathing in its glorious floods of light, seeing the sunbursts of morning among the icy peaks, the noonday radiance on the trees and rocks and snow, the flush of alpenglow and a thousand dashing waterfalls with their marvelous abundance of irised spray, it still seems to me above all others the Range of Light."* [5]

My head was literally in the clouds, though they were dark and furious. A small, rusty sign at the summit had *"Entering King's Canyon National Park"* painted on its north side and *"Entering Sequoia National Park"* on the other. I thirsted to explore the ridgeline and drink in the blissful panorama. But the strange weather intimidated me; plus, I relished the descent after three days of continuous climbing. Below me, warm, verdant slopes beckoned.

After three miles of steep switchbacks, the trail leveled out, but I began to wonder whether I could march two more miles to the Bearpaw Meadow campsite before dark. My canteen was less than half full, and the trail was now cutting across sheer granite cliffs above the Kaweah River.

Park regulations discourage and, in some places, forbid camping outside of designated sites in the backcountry. Not only is the mountain ecology fragile, but the canyons and meadows are ruled by black bears and mountain lions. Every night, hikers must suspend all their food, toothpaste, deodorant, ChapStick and sunblock in *bear bags* hung from the trees to discourage marauding predators. Throwing a sleeping bag down on the trail was not an option.

I scanned my topographic map for an alternate campsite. If I'd been willing to backtrack nearly a mile, Tamarack Lake Trail would've brought me to a shady flat beside Lone Pine Creek. But the sun had sunk behind the rough peaks, and their shadows stretched deep into the gorge. Onward or backward, neither option was appealing.

With only an hour of daylight to find a campsite, the adrenaline began to flow as the classic fight-or-flight response crept over me. The canyon walls seemed to slowly squeeze together. My attention narrowed. My breathing became more rapid. The wondrous beauty of the High Sierra Range was usurped by a single, definitive purpose — survival.

Pressured, though not yet desperate, I wondered, *"Why not take a shortcut?"* If I left the trail heading diagonally, cross-country, I'd probably reach the campsite before dark. I scanned the horizon for a tall, distinct mountain peak or outcropping to help me keep my bearings once I left the footpath.

"Why should I be afraid of something I know nothing about."

— Seneca

I stepped off the trail and headed for my landmark. The undergrowth was much heavier than I'd expected, and pushing through thickets of brush and chaparral frustrated my progress.

As I rushed forward, I ignored the ground getting softer and wetter — a kind of swampy bog I'd never encountered in the high country. My adrenalin levels were peaking and without ever deciding to do so, I found myself running. I had to get out of this swamp. I had to get to camp before dark. I had to run, run, run.

I don't think I ran more than 100 yards before a voice in the back of my head demanded my attention. *"Michael, something is very wrong here,"* it said. *"You're running through a swamp, crashing through brush with a 60-pound pack on your back. It's getting dark and you don't really know where you are. Stop, Michael. Just stop, now!"*

So I did. I stopped. The voice, however, continued. *"You're losing it, Michael. You're panicking. You're making things worse. Pull it together."*

I had practiced meditation and self-hypnosis for 10 years, so I knew how to use breathing to relax. For the next couple of minutes, I stood still, watching myself recover. Breathing slowly and deeply, I consciously felt my muscles relaxing, letting go of stress and tension.

Looking down at my feet, I found myself ankle-deep in muddy water. I almost laughed in relief as I realized what could've happened if I hadn't listened to that still, small voice in the back of my head.

I began to walk again, but now carefully and deliberately. Soon I realized I was closer to the campground than I'd feared. Wading the creek, I climbed up the bank to find the entire site vacant. I was tired, wet and still alone.

I filled my water bottle from the stream, lit my stove and made a cup of tea. Oddly, I wasn't very hungry, so I didn't eat much. Instead, I set up my tent, bear-bagged my supplies, hung them and pulled on my sleeping bag.

I slept in fits and starts that night. Residual adrenalin continued to race through my bloodstream. I knew how fortunate I was to have escaped my panic without getting hurt; but nevertheless, I was still wired and edgy. I was irritated when a majestic buck mule deer wandered into camp looking for handouts. Normally, I love watching these gentle high-country deer, but I tossed several pinches of gravel in its direction, hoping to be left alone.

It was the greatest fear I've ever felt, before or since. And I did it to myself. There was no danger, other than the danger my reflexive panic created — fear and anxiety born of what I did not understand about my situation and myself.

The Shadows of Fear

Fear is unsubstantial. It exists, but neither as force nor form. Just as darkness exists as the mere absence of light, fear is a lack of awareness. It's felt as the heartache, confusion and tension stimulated by unfamiliarity. Ignoring or denying fear further degrades awareness, intelligence and performance. Consciously facing fear is like turning on a powerful light that pierces the shadows to reveal the truth of things.

The common thread running through all problems is ignorance. You cannot reason with ignorance. It is irrational and frightening. But most people prefer the familiarity of their confusion and fear to the comfort and safety they do not know. And so their problems persist.

Many people mistake the underlying currents of anxiety in humans for evil, corruption or immorality. But it is unawareness, ignorance, confusion and fear. In all cultures and all times, wise women and men have encouraged us to defeat the wicked with goodness, to eradicate ignorance with understanding and to redeem fear and suffering with love.

Fear begs us for redemption. The more specific we can be about fear, the more personal it becomes; until at its core, we find fear thriving on our feeble and beleaguered sense of self. Those who ignore their fear and anxiety tend to interpret its vague, gnawing sensations as evidence they are truly alone and life is meaningless. But individuals who devote themselves to self-discovery soon recognize love and understanding as the antidote to fear and ignorance.

Love and fear work together. Like latitude and longitude, they are coordinates that reveal our position between what we understand and what we do *not* understand. Positive, love-based feelings encourage us to stay the course. Negative, fear-based feelings disclose the need for specific course corrections.

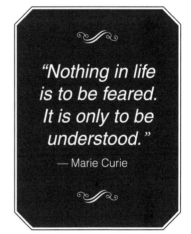

"Nothing in life is to be feared. It is only to be understood."

— Marie Curie

Pain and Discomfort Are Just Trying to Help

Heartache and upset serve the same function as physical pain. Aches and pain are clues — symptoms to help us identify and treat injury or illness. Emotional discomfort is no different. The full range of emotional hurt, despair, distress and dismay reveals a need to understand our self better.

We call fear-based feelings *negative emotions* only because they hurt, not because they are unhelpful. Fear is the common stimulus behind the entire set of hurtful emotions. Rather than wishing we could abolish fear, we must redeem it with self-awareness, meaning insight and understanding.

Any disinterest in exploring our individuality compounds our fear of the unknown as it struggles with the fear of inadequacy, intimacy and change.

The fear of social rejection battles with primal fears of being alone. The fear of dying is one side of our fear of living fully, much like the twin fears of success and failure. When our fear of self-awareness prevents us from looking deeper, it develops into vicious cycles of escalating fear and self-ignorance.

We give away our power whenever we rely on the acceptance of others while blaming them for our discontent. We cannot heal what we refuse to feel and accept as our personal responsibility.

Nothing of value can come from playing the victim. Both emotional and physical feelings are personal responses to the stimulus of life. A willingness to be accountable for our emotions, thoughts and behavior boosts personal power, effectiveness and overall happiness.

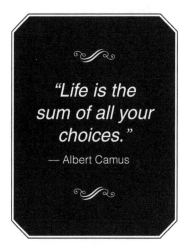

"Life is the sum of all your choices."
— Albert Camus

Fear has many names, expressing itself as routine stress, non-specific anxiety, worry, nervousness, apprehension, dread, panic, terror, paranoia, anxiety disorders including post-traumatic stress (PTSD), obsessive-compulsive disorder (OCD), attention deficit hyperactivity disorder (ADHD), numerous sleep and eating disorders, most forms of depression and a broad variety of phobias.

There are hundreds of names for the emotional heartache and dismay born of that fear, though the most common include sadness, anger, hate, contempt, grief, suspicion, disgust and humiliation. Every emotional feeling that hurts, upsets, frustrates or irritates us contains hidden gifts. By developing self-awareness, we can propagate the innate seeds of wisdom encased by our heartache.

Separated, Afraid and Alone in the Unknown

Few situations are more frightening than feeling abandoned, separated and alone. The trauma of birth starts a process of individuation that contributes to a lifetime of alienation and anxiety, even with the best parenting. In their earliest months, infants begin to realize they have detached from their mothers. Over time, as mom comes and goes and various objects vanish and return, a child's separation of self from the external world intensifies.

This subject-object split quickly expands from mom-or-me to them-or-us, and soon we presume differences are always opposites. Many adults retain these infantile, all-or-nothing presumptions, as if anything that's not 100% true must be completely false. Situations are seen as either good or bad. If someone is not with you, they must be against you.

Rooted in the limbic brain's fight-or-flight reflex, these polarized thought-patterns — false dichotomies, binarisms, bifurcation fallacies — are compounded by routine anxiety and reinforced by the apparent duality in gender, magnetic polarity and the vibrating, cyclic nature of all energy.

Reflexive *"you or me"* belief systems aggravate unawareness, confusion, stress, anxiety and fear. Further, the appearance of separation — each of us living in unique and disconnected bodies — supports our feelings of alienation and victimization. It is the insecure animal in us, not the self-aware human that bites the rock thrown at us.

"Lovely days don't come to you, you should walk to them."
— Rumi

No Edges, No Separation

The separate and distinct appearance of material forms is also an illusion. Even the densest elements have no edges and are less compact than a snowstorm.

Matter is condensed energy ($E=mc^2$), so every separate particle is actually an integral part of One Cosmic Energy Field. The Universe is an inconceivably vast ocean of potential energy in various states — gravity, electromagnetism, nuclear, plasma, gas, liquid and solids.

Nobel Prize-winning physicist Eugene Vigner said, *"It was not possible to formulate the laws of quantum mechanics in a fully consistent way without reference to the consciousness ... The content of the consciousness is the ultimate universal reality."* And the brilliant physicist Max Planck admits, *"Science cannot solve the ultimate mystery of nature because, in the last analysis, we ourselves are a part of the mystery that we are trying to solve."*

Even more simply, another Nobel Prize winner in physics, Erwin Schrödinger, has written, *"Quantum physics thus reveals a basic oneness of the universe .... Multiplicity is only apparent. In truth, there is only one mind."*[6]

What is there to fear, if there's only One of us here? Philosophers and theologians have numerous names for the Unified Energy Field — God, Holy Spirit, Love, Awareness, consciousness, panpsychism and monism. The inseparability of energy, spirit and matter is also described as non-dualism and non-duality. It is the Kingdom within and around us, connecting everything to every other thing — the still, silent Love that brings forth and sustains all Life.

Defining organic life has proven to be exceedingly difficult. The brains of mammals are more complex than those of reptiles or insects, and clearly some animals are more self-aware than others. But it appears all life forms are conscious.

The plant kingdom is self-replicative and responsive to its environment. Paramecium and amoebae exhibit a rudimentary aptitude in their ability to learn and remember. There's a wealth of nascent research about the intelligence demonstrated by single-celled Protista — a kingdom of organisms that is not animal, plant nor fungi. Even the slime-mold physarum has been shown to solve the shortest-path problem when hunting for food hidden by researchers in tiny mazes.[7]

The One and the Many

Western mystics use the phrase, *"the One and the Many,"* to explain physical creatures as diverse yet inalienable extensions, fragments or facets of a single Source.[8] Eastern scholars often refer to a two-truth doctrine, acknowledging the relative truth of matter appearing as separate forms, plus the Absolute Truth of non-duality.

Further, consciousness is viewed as relative, while Awareness is understood to be Absolute. The teacher Nisargadatta Maharaj said, *"Awareness is Absolute. Consciousness is relative to its content. Consciousness is always of something. Consciousness is partial and changeful. Awareness is total, changeless, calm and silent. And it is the common matrix of every experience."*

Imagine flying through interstellar space on a small asteroid. Your spacesuit provides all the air, water and nutrition you need to survive. Suddenly, the asteroid splits in half. Would you need to hold on? And if the asteroid shattered into a dozen or a thousand pieces, would holding on change anything?

Of course not, because you and the asteroid would continue to float through space at a meaningless speed, except relative to some other object in space. There is no up or down, no forward or back, no left or right in deep space. But our instincts tell us to hold on for dear life. Like riding a roller coaster, we hold on if we're afraid, but when excited, we let go and raise our hands above our heads.

Fear and excitement are similar feelings — weak knees, girded loins, butterflies in the stomach, heart palpitations, lump in the throat and sweaty palms. Reflexive tension aggravates fear. Letting go of those same feelings fosters excitement that motivates us onward and upward. Humanistic and transpersonal academics suggest we emancipate fear and ignorance with love and understanding — initially as self-awareness, followed by empathy and compassion for others.

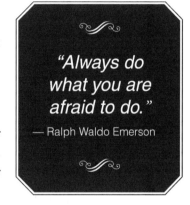

"Always do what you are afraid to do."

— Ralph Waldo Emerson

Holy Holism

Meticulous scientific examinations of Nature reveal endless patterns of harmony and unity in all things. The inter-reliance of the animal, plant and mineral kingdoms supports the ancient monistic theories about the non-dual synergy of the environment.

Ecologists credit the philosopher Jan Christian Smuts with having coined the term *"holism"* in 1926 as the inter-reliance of Nature began receiving wide acceptance. Later, the philosopher-architect R. Buckminster Fuller wrote at length about Nature developing synergistic systems in which parts work together to produce better results than the sum of those parts. In his 1981 book *Critical Path*, Fuller wrote, *"There are no solids. There are no things. There are only interfering and non-interfering patterns operative in pure principle, and principles are eternal. Principles never contradict principles … The synergetic integral of the totality of principles is God."*

Fear is born of our failure to recognize the Universe as an integrated whole system, as if *"This one is not that one, and I am not that."* Though novel to most Westerners, a core principle of Eastern philosophy from the ancient Upanishads is, *"Tat Tvam Asi,"*[9] meaning, *"You are That,"* and consequently, the appearance of separation is an illusion.

The Basics of Fear and Heartache

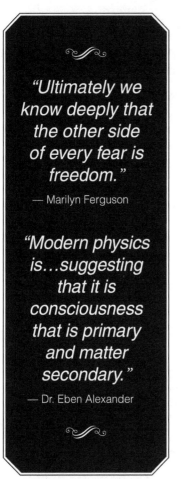

"Ultimately we know deeply that the other side of every fear is freedom."

— Marilyn Ferguson

"Modern physics is...suggesting that it is consciousness that is primary and matter secondary."

— Dr. Eben Alexander

All fear is *"fear of the unknown."* Most people not only fear what they don't understand about themselves, but also are frightened of understanding themselves better.

Fear runs the gamut from terror and panic to nervous worry and mild apprehension. Most dictionaries define fear as uncomfortable, tense feelings triggered by danger, real or imagined. But more precisely, fear indicates confusion, ignorance and a lack of awareness or understanding.

Fear always highlights some lack of self-awareness, regardless of whether it includes an external threat. It is an internal signal that urges us to seek greater understanding of the world within and around us. In this sense, our personal fear is a friend and ally, becoming a painful problem only when ignored or denied. Fearlessness is not unawareness, rejection or denial of fear, but rather the willingness to intimately embrace everything unknown, so we may learn, understand and evolve.

Some of my students and clients object to this concept, insisting that spiders, snakes, tornadoes and earthquakes, for example, are frightening because they are dangerous. I won't deny that fear can be an instinctive reaction to danger — real or imagined. But in either case, fear is a direct reflection of what we do not understand. The better we understand dangerous threats, the less we fear them.

Since fear originates in unawareness, ignorance and confusion, it's most evident when there's no reason for it. This condition is called *free-floating* or *non-specific anxiety*. Many people suffer from the false narrative that fear protects them — that expecting the worst will somehow help them more carefully avoid it. But this misconception is contradicted by three widely accepted axioms — the Law of Attraction, *"You get what you expect;"* target fixation, *"You go where you look;"* and karma, *"You reap what you sow."*

Pessimists defend their negativity as *"realistic."* Ironically, they generate evidence that their futility is justified; just as disorganized thinkers foster chaos and optimists produce positive outcomes. Life is a self-fulfilling prophecy.

Americans are especially disposed to externalizing their fear. There are more guns in the U.S. than people — 50% more per capita than any other nation. Half of all guns in America are owned by just 3% of the population, while more than two-thirds of Americans are unarmed and unafraid.[10] Despite a significant drop in violent crime, a 2016 study by Harvard and Northeastern universities determined that the fear of other people had become the primary motive for gun ownership in the U.S., a radical shift from a 1994 report showing most guns were purchased for hunting and sport shooting.[11]

> *"Every particular in nature, a leaf, a drop, a crystal, a moment of time is related to the whole, and partakes of the perfection of the whole."*
>
> — Dr. Eben Alexander

> *"We fear things in proportion to our ignorance of them."*
>
> — Titus Livius Patavinus

There are violent criminals and terrorists in the world, but fear lives within us. It's always smarter to manage our irrational fear than the imaginary danger we project on others.

Evidence of fear's irrationality is easy to find. Many parents use fear of the bogeyman to keep their children in bed at night. Millions of people refuse to swim in the ocean due to their fear of shark attack. Globally, five to 10 people per year die from shark attacks, though mosquito bites kill up to one million people annually. And few people fear mosquitoes.

Fear of flying is another example of unwarranted anxiety. Statistically, we're much safer in an airplane than in a car. Airplane crashes are rare, while automobile accidents kill 30,000 to 40,000 Americans each year. And some true dangers don't feel frightening at all — slip-and-fall accidents, cigarettes, alcohol, pharmaceuticals and high-fat foods.

Facts have little or no influence over those who suffer from irrational phobias. Some phobia will distress nearly one in 10 Americans in their lifetime. Although the complex causes of phobias, panic attacks, obsessive-compulsive disorder (OCD) and general anxiety disorders are not well understood, most researchers agree both genetics and environment are factors.[12]

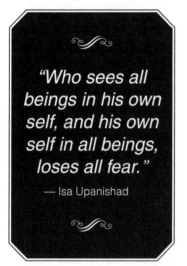

"Who sees all beings in his own self, and his own self in all beings, loses all fear."

— Isa Upanishad

The Subjectivity of Fear-based Emotions

Despite appearances, the world is now safer than it's ever been.[13] In those rare instances when we are confronted by real, clear and present danger, our fear says little or nothing about the danger itself. Instead, fearful responses point to our unawareness, confusion and misunderstandings about our vulnerability.

The best way to manage fear, whether or not it's related to danger, is to confront and explore it intuitively. As you'll see in later chapters, **Fearless Intelligence** provides techniques and instruction to face fear and appreciate the insight and understanding concealed within it.

Fear is not a single emotion. It is the common thread running through *all hurt and upset* — anger, sadness, distrust, disgust, envy, irritation, frustration, desperation, humiliation, heartache and confusion. Often, we feel a combination of several emotions simultaneously, which adds to our confusion. Unlike thoughts, which are heard and pictured in the mind, emotions are felt in the physical body, mostly in the core between the heart and abdomen. Sometimes the upper and lower extremities are involved, as in flushed cheeks, sweaty palms, girded loins or weak knees.

Besides the brain's basic aptitude for logic, there are three other nerve plexuses (braided networks) that provide non-logical information to the brain. The cardiac plexus at the base of the heart has long been associated with positive emotions and intuition, while the sacral plexuses correspond to hurtful emotions, instinct and reflexive behavior. These two plexuses overlap and share the belly's solar plexus, which communicates directly with the brain through the vagus (pneumogastric) nerve.

Commonly, the words *intuition* and *instinct* are mistakenly conflated. Sometimes called *the sixth sense,* neither is actually a sense. Instead, intuition and instinct are two forms of non-logical intelligence — not illogical, but complementary alternatives to deductive reasoning.

The Symptom Is Not the Problem

Semanticist Alfred Korzybski (1879-1950) wrote, *"The map is not the territory,"* as a way of explaining that words are symbols of the meanings they represent. An ancient example can be found in the Buddhist sutra that says, *"The finger pointing at the moon is not the moon."* Our perception of reality is biased by the stories we tell ourselves. Typically, the personal narratives that define us are dreadful compared to what's really happening.

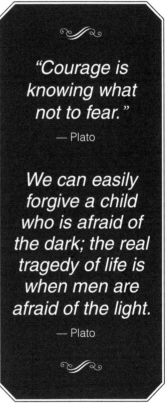

"Courage is knowing what not to fear."
— Plato

We can easily forgive a child who is afraid of the dark; the real tragedy of life is when men are afraid of the light.
— Plato

The hurt caused by fear-based emotions is a symptom of complex underlying anxieties. Pain, whether emotional or physical, points to more elusive disorders that need insight and understanding to be relieved.

When the alternator warning light on your car's dashboard lights up, you don't replace the light. Instead, you open the hood and test the alternator, voltage regulator, drive belt and battery. When your gas gauge nears the empty mark, you don't repair the gauge; you add gas. Emotions are your brain's dashboard.

Concealing your car's dashboard won't prevent problems. In the same way, gobbling down opioids to block physical pain or antidepressants to disregard emotional distress can be just as misguided, especially for extended periods.

So instead of repressing anger with a third beer, ask yourself *why* you're so angry. Rather than insulting a waitress over poorly prepared food, consider *why* you've been feeling irritable all day. And when you shout, *"Look what you made me do,"* pause and accept responsibility for your actions.

Some small portion of our despair and discontent reflects what we do not understand about the world. But the bulk of our emotional pain is symptomatic of our failure to understand our true character and the emotional feelings it produces. As we understand the significance of our emotional heartache and anxiety, it stops. It simply vanishes as self-awareness expands.

To summarize, **Fearless Intelligence** includes four critical principles:

1. Fear and anxiety are reactions to whatever we do not understand about our situation and our self, whether dangerous or not.

2. Our hurtful emotions are symptoms of fear and anxiety — all sadness, dismay, despair, heartache, frustration, irritation and humiliation.

3. The antidote is awareness — understanding both our self-worth and the hidden meanings of our emotional discomfort.

4. Awareness can be learned through stress reduction and mindfulness.

In Plato's classic *Allegory of the Cave*, men who have spent countless years imprisoned in a deep, dark cavern are terrified by the bright colors and clearly defined forms when they break out into the full light of day. They hurry back into the cave, where they find comfort in the familiarity of shadow and muted shades of gray — prisoners of their fear and ignorance.

Our fear and unawareness are like the leg collar and chain once used to restrain baby circus elephants. Even after adult elephants are strong enough to easily break their restraints, they no longer try. They remain bound — not by the chains, but by their limited beliefs.

Awareness Is Mindful Detachment

Just as we can ponder conflicting thoughts without committing to one or another, we can better understand our fear and hurtful emotions from a detached, elevated perspective. A simple definition of this mindfulness is *to be aware of the present moment without judgment.* Or said another way, *to relax and passively watch your thoughts and feelings unfold without scrutiny, deliberation or labeling.*

Mindful detachment provides us with an expanded overview, as if stepping back or rising above our emotions to see the bigger picture. Emotions are like water, turning opaque when disturbed, yet transparent when still. As mindfulness calms our emotions, we can peer into their depths and see our overshadowing spiritual values reflected on the surface.

For example, imagine seeing your own anger coming toward you — still small and on the horizon, but growing. You might think, *"If I don't do something soon, I'll become angry and react in ways I'll later regret."*

Being aware of our anger helps us avoid the victimization and helplessness of *"getting angry."* An awareness of the hurt and fear behind anger can reveal *why* we're upset — a realization that permits us to choose more appropriate responses. Such insight requires us to view our emotional feelings as personal reactions. People who see themselves as victims of their hurt and upset are unlikely to consider the valuable insight they contain.

> *"If someone comes along and shoots an arrow into your heart, it's fruitless to stand there and yell at the person. It would be much better to turn your attention to the fact that there's an arrow in your heart."*
> — Pema Chodron

While the adages *"Think twice"* and *"On second thought"* have multiple meanings, consider the benefits of double-checking your impulsive thoughts and feelings before reacting. In a refined sense, a *second thought* is not merely an additional thought, but an opportunity to gain an elevated perspective — an opening to see whether we're truly aware of the consequences of reacting too quickly to our thoughts and feelings.

Awareness can be learned with stress reduction and mindfulness. The skill of developing self-awareness-on-demand is called mindfulness-based stress reduction (MBSR). With the exercises detailed in this book, you can develop an ability to shift at will to an objective understanding of your emotions. Instead of acting like a helpless victim, you can mindfully step back, expand your self-awareness and make conscious choices about your attitudes and responses.

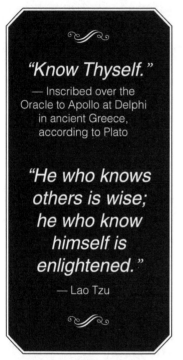

"Know Thyself."
— Inscribed over the Oracle to Apollo at Delphi in ancient Greece, according to Plato

"He who knows others is wise; he who know himself is enlightened."
— Lao Tzu

The Blame Game

Fear is difficult to understand because not understanding can be frightening — whether new or old, unknown or known. How often have you asked yourself, *"What am I afraid of?"* before realizing you have no idea. You simply feel afraid, nervous, stressed or apprehensive for no apparent reason. And that's the point. Whenever we're confused, uninformed or unaware, fear alerts us, whether dangerous or not.

Blaming people who frustrate and irritate us provides no advantage or benefit. The world in which we live is not the real cause of frustration. We only appear to be targets, victims or effects of a life done to us. We can always choose our point of view and initiate an appropriate response.

Imagine a friend playfully poking you where you're already bruised. You cry out, *"Hey, that hurt!"* But the person who poked you becomes defensive and says, *"No, that shouldn't have hurt you."*

You reply, *"Yes, it did hurt. You poked me where I was already bruised and it really hurt."*

58

To which the other person counters, *"Well, then, I didn't hurt you. You were already hurt."*

And, of course, both things are true — your friend *did* hurt you, but only because you were already injured. We all carry old emotional bruises from childhood and adolescence — emotional wounds that never fully healed and frequently hurt when others unknowingly arouse them.

This explains why negative emotions often seem misdirected and out of proportion. The conditions that irritate us often aggravate old, unresolved heartache. Once we accept our emotions as personal responses, we can recognize them as symptoms of our confusion. Expanding self-awareness with stress reduction exposes the reasons we suffer. And the insight and understanding that follow set us free from our fear and ignorance.

Exercises:

Remember a time when you were afraid, but didn't know why. Close your eyes, relax and ask yourself, *"Was I in any real danger at the time?"* If not, what did that particular fear represent? What did you learn about yourself?

Recall a recent occasion when you were angry or depressed. Was there any fear in those feelings? What did you learn about yourself?

CHAPTER 4 —
WHAT IS THE WISDOM
OF MINDFULNESS?

Beyond knowledge, wisdom understands cause, meaning, ethics and application, plus a sense of what we do not know.

During my career as a broadcast journalist and radio talk show host in Detroit and Los Angeles, I became intrigued by the distinctions around opinion, belief, knowledge and understanding. I found most opinions are based on anecdotal experience and limited knowledge. Further, belief systems are often distorted by a need to be right rather than a devoted search for truth. So, opinions may be part of a serious attempt to discern the facts, or more often than not, a personal defense mechanism.

Of even greater interest to me, however, is the difference between knowledge and understanding. Einstein is quoted as having said, *"Any fool can know. The point is to understand."* Knowledge is accumulated information. However, understanding suggests an awareness of cause, meaning and application. Collecting, storing and sharing information is a simple task. It is much more difficult to stockpile and communicate understanding.

In the early 1990s, I formed a small networking group called *Individuals Making a Difference* (IMAD) for progressive activists. Our main agenda was supporting people of conscience, no matter their issue. We met in a small coffee shop called the *Sunshine Cafe* in the L.A. suburb of Glendale. Attendance rarely exceeded two- or three-dozen people, but the group was well known because our discussion points often came up on my KLSX-FM talk show.

One evening, a surprising incident showed me the difference between knowledge and understanding. Four young men joined us who no one recognized. They sat together quietly in the back of the room. After several of our regulars announced their activities and events, one of the strangers raised his hand. I welcomed him to our meeting, asking what project he and his friends were working on, and how we might help them.

I didn't recognize the name of the group he gave us. It sounded like some ad hoc committee supporting people displaced from low-income housing by an urban renewal project. But his announcement of an upcoming street protest was loaded with harsh, confrontational rhetoric.

They promised to *challenge* the police on this and *confront* the city council on that and *force* people to accept such and such. I asked him if his group had a permit to demonstrate with the march and rally they had scheduled. He insisted their First Amendment rights superseded the need for any city permits.

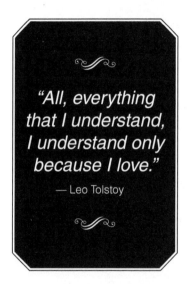

"All, everything that I understand, I understand only because I love."

— Leo Tolstoy

Gesturing toward the larger group, I said, *"Well, you folks do as you please, but I think these guys are cops. They're LAPD provocateurs."*

Agent Provocateurs

As a journalist, I was aware of the Los Angeles Police Department's *Red Squad* — a holdover from the Communist witch-hunts of the McCarthy Era. Officially dubbed the *Public Disorder Intelligence Division* (PDID), local police not only gathered intelligence on social and political activists but also infiltrated the leadership of these groups.

A paid police informant named Cheryl Bell became president of the antiwar group, *The Alliance for Survival,* in the early '80s. Another contracted informant, Connie Milazzo, ingratiated herself into the leadership of the *L.A. Coalition Against Police Abuse* (CAPA). Sworn LAPD officers also infiltrated and spied on the United Farm Workers (UFW) and Vietnam Veterans Against the War (VVAW). PDID even spied on elected members of the L.A. City Council and groups working to integrate public schools.

In 1961, Frank Wilkinson, the founder of the National Committee to Abolish HUAC (the House Un-American Activities Committee), was imprisoned for one year in an Atlanta jail for refusing to testify to Senator Joe McCarthy's infamous commie-hunters. Twenty years later on my KLOS-FM talk show, Wilkinson said he was certain the FBI had *not* spied on him. But through a petition filed in 1986 under the Freedom of Information Act (FOIA), Wilkinson received over 132,000 pages of FBI files about his anti-HUAC activities. The mostly inaccurate information had been gathered under J. Edgar Hoover's illegal counterintelligence program known to secret agents as COINTELPRO.

The FBI spied on U.S. Senators who opposed the war in Vietnam, including Howard Baker (R-Tenn.) and Frank Church (D-Idaho), civil rights leaders, journalists, outspoken athletes and rock stars. Further, federal agents posing as activists infiltrated the American Civil Liberties Union (ACLU), the Black Panthers, the American Indian Movement (AIM) and community church groups like the Quakers and Unitarians for their anti-war efforts. Secret FBI files were even maintained on the eminent scientist Albert Einstein — a socialist, pacifist and civil rights activist — even before COINTELPRO was launched in 1956.

> *"The whole aim of practical politics is to keep the populace alarmed — and hence clamorous to be led to safety — by menacing it with an endless series of hobgoblins, all of them imaginary."*
> — H.L. Mencken

In 2008, the ACLU collected evidence of Denver undercover police instigating violence at the Democratic National Convention to disrupt and discredit protestors.[14] Four years earlier, there were similar allegations that New York City undercover police staged attacks on their uniformed colleagues at the Republican National Convention.[15]

In 2014, U.S. Senator Dianne Feinstein (D-Calif.) publicly accused the CIA of illegal spying on the Senate Intelligence Committee's investigation of CIA torture during the U.S. overthrow of Iraq's Saddam Hussein. At first, CIA Director John Brennan vehemently denied the accusation. However, he soon admitted having lied and formally apologized to committee leaders.

Back at the Sunshine Cafe

A collective gasp had sucked the air out of the restaurant's small meeting room. Three or four long seconds ticked by before the silence was broken by the timid, awkward denials of our visitors. There was no outrage — none of the indignity the situation might have called for. The previously bold radical leader suddenly found himself off-script with no retorts or ad-libs. He stuttered and stammered while nervously shifting his weight from one foot to the other.

> "The government has granted itself power it is not entitled to. There is no public oversight ... The vast majority of human communications are automatically ingested without targeting."
>
> — Edward Snowden

Realizing they wouldn't be recruiting anyone that night, the four men shuffled out the door. After a brief discussion, we took a break. Two or three of our regulars stepped outside for a cigarette but returned quickly to tell us the infiltrators were still in the parking lot writing license plate numbers on note pads.

Understanding Beyond Knowledge

Those undercover police were collecting *"intelligence"* — information or knowledge about our group. As often happens when institutions gather data, their knowledge did not extend to understanding the meaning or motivation of our mission. Bureaucracies are not known for their insight or wisdom.

I exposed the impostors with no specific *knowledge* about them because of my radio talk show and counseling experience with deceptive people. Intuitive understanding transcends knowledge. Known also as expanded awareness, higher consciousness and metacognition, wisdom includes our capacity to think about thinking, to be aware of self-awareness and consider all that remains unknown.

The seeds of this self-awareness and emotional intelligence book, *Fearless Intelligence*, began in 2013 as a one-day training commissioned by the Orange County California Sheriff's Academy. The job responsibilities of police, deputies, marshals and agents all across the U.S. have become so complex and comprehensive that new levels of professionalism are required from cadets through the ranks to top administrators.

In his book, *"Police Suicide: Epidemic in Blue,"* John Violanti, a professor of epidemiology at the University of Buffalo, writes: *"Police officers … tend to have higher rates of alcohol use than many other professions."* [16] A study commissioned in 2009 by the Badge of Life Police Mental Health Foundation documented 143 police suicides in the U.S., nearly *"three times the number of officers killed by felons."* Alcohol abuse was identified as the predominant factor. An update in 2016 revealed a 24% reduction in police suicide, primarily due to a transition from suicide prevention programs to broader mental health intervention by outside trainers.

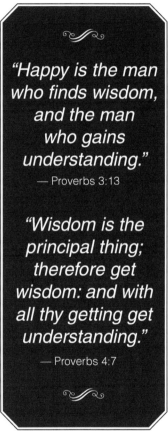

"Happy is the man who finds wisdom, and the man who gains understanding."
— Proverbs 3:13

"Wisdom is the principal thing; therefore get wisdom: and with all thy getting get understanding."
— Proverbs 4:7

While stress and anxiety have countless sources, the common thread is a lack of self-awareness. An often-hostile *siege mentality* can develop and become reinforced when police and sheriff's academy graduates are required to staff jails for as long as five years before being assigned to street patrols. Training in stress reduction, emotional intelligence and empathy is needed to build self-awareness and proper social skills.

Acknowledging Understanding to Others

The two most effective skills for managing relationships are attentive listening and verbal acknowledgment. Many people in positions of authority are unwilling to say, *"I understand how you feel."* They fear inferences of agreement or acquiescence. Even the phrase, *"That may be,"* is often avoided out of a concern it may be perceived as submissive.

During one of my first classes for deputies and jail staff at the Orange County California Sheriff's Academy, a young deputy in the back row raised his hand to say, *"Sir, excuse me, but I have no desire to tell some inmate that I*

understand how he feels. I expect him to do what I tell him to do because I say so."
My response was, *"Yes sir, I absolutely understand how you feel."*

Of course, everyone had a good laugh — not derisive laughter, but the good-hearted recognition of just how effective and authoritative acknowledgment can be. The technique we teach is a variation on a well-known sales skill referred to as *Feel, Felt, Found.* Instead of trying to undermine or overcome customer objections, smart salespeople will imply agreement by saying, *"Yes, I understand how you feel. In fact, I've felt that way myself, but here's what I've found ..."*

The law enforcement version is a little different. We teach officers and staff to listen respectfully to the complaint or objection and then say: *"Yes, I understand how you feel. If I were in your position, I might feel the same way. However, here's what we need to do ..."*

Arguments are not contests or competitions we win or lose. Wars of words are battles for understanding, not conquest or agreement. Though surprising to many, we can resolve a great deal of discord without concession by understanding and acknowledging the views of those with whom we disagree.

The DIKW Hierarchy

Exploding computer technology in the 1980s fostered the creation of a model known as the *Wisdom Pyramid* or *DIKW Hierarchy* – data, information, knowledge and wisdom. Often attributed to American organizational theorist Russell Ackoff, this pyramid shows a grading of understanding.

At the base of the pyramid, we find data — raw statistics, markers and measurements. These values can be numbers, words or simple phrases. The second step is information, which is data organized into a particular sequence, like a sentence or equation. Knowledge is information learned from education and experience put into context. And wisdom is the comprehended significance of knowledge — insight about motives, causes and effects, applications,

EVOLUTION OF UNDERSTANDING ramifications and implications —

Wisdom

Knowledge

Information

Data

plus an awareness of what remains unknown.

In ancient times, wisdom was the awareness of spiritual Love between God and humanity that surpasses knowledge.[17] Wisdom transcends knowledge in five ways — cause, meaning, application, ethics and mysteries.

Cause

Aristotle described wisdom as *understanding causes* — the reasons *why* things happen and exist as they do. He termed the composition of things *material cause.* Actions, he said, are *efficient causes,* and interactions are *formal causes.* And the ultimate purpose of things he called the *final cause.*

Unlike Europe's 18th century Age of Enlightenment, based on reason and empirical science, enlightenment in Eastern philosophy is wisdom — the ultimate spiritual awareness or highest level of consciousness. Various traditions use terms like satori, prajna, kensho and moksha to mean wisdom, insight and the understanding of one's true essence. From this perspective, wisdom views the appearance of all material separation as scattered reflections or fragments of a single Cause or spiritual Source extending beyond the boundaries of time and space.

Ironically, the semantics of *final cause* includes *first cause,* also known as the causeless cause, the unmoved mover or the Absolute. After first cause, everything exists as part of a causal chain of interactions. As the French Catholic philosopher Sertillanges has written, *"Everything we experience appears to belong to a chain of existing things … which cross and interlace, indefinitely sub-divided into a number of combinations, but where everything is linked up. One being comes from another, which itself finds its raison d'etre in a third, and this third in another. An effect comes from a cause, which in turn implies a third."*[18]

Meaning

Secondly, wisdom offers meaning. While knowledge may outline the *basic* meaning of information, wisdom enlarges that meaning with insight, implications and consequences.

Knowledge helps us identify the central elements of inquiry, answering who, what, where, when and how (how much). Wisdom expands knowledge to include the more substantial meaning of things — the *why* or *why not,* the motives and ideals.[19]

Julius Caesar was the first to proclaim, *"Experience is the teacher of all things,"* which is especially true for understanding the full meaning of things. For example, being told not to run into the street doesn't guarantee children will understand *why* it's dangerous.

One day, in a playful burst of enthusiasm, little Billy chases his ball into the street. The driver of an unseen car slams on his brakes, screeching to a halt, just in time to avoid smashing into the boy.

Billy is traumatized but safe, and now understands *why* he shouldn't run into the street. Sometimes it takes a real-world experience to elevate knowledge to a rich and meaningful understanding.

Application

Thirdly, understanding includes recognition of how to apply our knowledge. Bucky Fuller was fond of saying, *"Humanity is acquiring all the right technology for all the wrong reasons."* Consumer technology in the Computer Age is less about solving real problems than delivering products we didn't know we needed, like Wi-Fi refrigerators and washing machines, smart hairbrushes, Amazon's Dash buttons and the Apple watch. Sure, they're fun and sometimes convenient, but they fail to enrich our lives in any meaningful way.

Smartphones are mini-computers that can perform billions of calculations per second. But besides an occasional phone call, we primarily use them to send brief text messages, play digital music and snap selfies. The Internet has wired the world, but we haven't come close to using our collective knowledge to its highest and best potential — to reverse the impact of greenhouse gases on climate change, to feed and house those in extreme poverty, to abolish racism, war, capital punishment, animal cruelty and to regulate *"winner take all"* capitalism for the greater good of all.

Ethics

Fourthly, wisdom includes moral and ethical principles. Just as the word *Love* in the Hebrew Bible embraces wisdom, understanding and awareness, the word *heart* signifies the phenomenon of human conscience.[20] In the earliest epistles of the New Testament, St. Paul repeatedly used the word *conscience*, from the Latin *conscientem*, meaning to *be aware* or *to know thoroughly.*[21]

Rarely does logical knowledge imply any ethical sense of right or wrong, guilt, anguish, enlightenment or high-minded moral principles. Conscience, however, is a non-logical, often spontaneous opening to emotional and spiritual realizations of moral and ethical principles.

Mysteries

And lastly, while knowledge is, by definition, limited to what's known, wisdom contains awareness of what is *not* known. This may be the primary virtue of wisdom — the understanding that there is always more to learn. Wisdom requires us to see past our fear of the unknown. The Sufi mystic Rumi described it as, *"…looking at the thorn and seeing the rose, looking at the night and seeing the day … (to) know that the moon needs time to become full."*

Fear is the feeling of not understanding something, whether or not we know it. So we must confront our fear and all of its symptoms — anger, sadness, heartache, frustration and confusion — to become more aware of what anxiety and stress represent.

Understanding heals by permitting us to release our ignorance, confusion and unawareness. Imagine how different the world will be once some significant number of us realizes we can release fear and ignorance, rather than conquer our muddled illusions of danger.

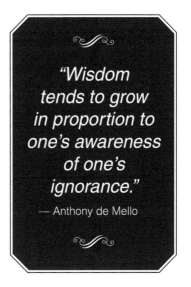

"Wisdom tends to grow in proportion to one's awareness of one's ignorance."

— Anthony de Mello

Knowing *what* we fear is a good start, but to resolve fear we must fully understand *why* something frightens us. Ralph Waldo Emerson wrote, *"Knowledge is the antidote to fear."* He would have been more precise if he had said, *"Understanding is the antidote to fear."*

Plato recalled Socrates explaining his reputation as a wise person by stating, *"I am better off than he is — for he knows nothing and thinks that he knows. I neither know nor think that I know."* In another fragment, Plato quotes his mentor as saying, *"I appear to be wiser than he, because I do not fancy I know what I do not know."*

There are four basic reasons self-aware people are better at distinguishing their knowledge from everything that remains unknown:

1. They are fearless — unafraid to face and accept what they do not know.

2. They continually review their belief systems and release subjective biases — labels, expectation and judgment, which distort and obstruct awareness.

3. They seek Truth over a desire for approval, orthodoxy or control.

4. Above all, they are true to themselves, yet humble, kind and compassionate.

The Amygdala Hijack

Facing the unknown is challenging. The *fight or flight* reflex has evolved as the brain's way of boosting physical strength and endurance whenever we feel afraid, stressed or confused. However, there is a trade-out for this survival response — a significant restriction of self-awareness and loss of mental and emotional intelligence. Whether practiced while wide-awake or in more focused states of meditation, mindfulness enhances awareness and intelligence by reversing the limbic brain's unconscious fight-or-flight response.

Whenever we feel afraid or just confused, an area of the ancient limbic brain called the *amygdala* elevates pulse, blood pressure, respiration, muscular tension and levels of the hormones adrenaline, cortisol and norepinephrine. Further, the amygdala disables the centers of reasoning and awareness in the neocortex to prevent the nuances of logic from slowing down reaction time.

The limbic brain cannot distinguish between fear of the unknown and real, imminent danger. As a result, our mental and emotional intelligence often gets hijacked when we need it most. Because natural selection favored the primitive humans who reacted without reasoning, their offspring to this day have inherited traits for becoming less aware and less intelligent when stressed for any reason.

Earth is safer now than ever before, but humans still carry the hair-triggers of their fearful ancestors. And though less dangerous, our daily problems have become more complex. Increasingly, our personal and social survival depends on expanded awareness, instead of physical strength and endurance. Mindfulness practices develop the awareness and equanimity needed to distinguish the fear of ignorance and confusion from the fear of actual danger.

The Mindful Awareness of Wisdom

It is often said that unlike knowledge, wisdom cannot be taught — that a person must be wise to appreciate wisdom. Yet those who would rather understand than be right can cultivate a mindful awareness of wisdom through insight meditation, also called vipassana.

Do not confuse concentration with mindfulness. Concentration requires single-pointed attention while attempting to suppress and ignore all distraction. The objective of mindfulness is to remain aware of distractions while refusing the temptation to judge or evaluate any of it.

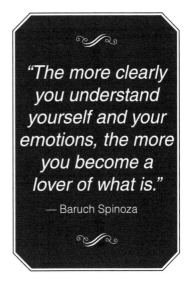

"The more clearly you understand yourself and your emotions, the more you become a lover of what is."

— Baruch Spinoza

Empirical research shows mindfulness meditators to be more self-aware than those who practice concentration.[22] Mindfulness meditation usually begins with a focus on the cyclic nature of involuntary breathing. Variations include watching one's meandering thought-stream or the ebb and flow of sensations in the body — emotional and physical. The intention of mindfulness is to observe each passing moment with curiosity and wonder, but without judgment, labeling or anticipation.

Instead of trying to inhibit distraction or rebuke yourself when concentration breaks, mindfulness meditators accept the inevitability of scattered attention and acknowledge it as soon as possible. Meditators soon realize their awareness can remain unbroken, even though their trains of thought may leap from track to track.

Over time, we can attain an exalted view of being the observer of our thoughts, rather than the thinker — or worse, a victim of our thinking.

Self-observation in calm, relaxed states produces the freedom to encourage thoughts and feelings that benefit us, while releasing those that don't.

Whether non-directed or contemplative, mindfulness meditation is simply a practice of detaching from the mind's perpetual thought streams and stepping back to a place of expanded objective awareness — a moment-to-moment comprehension of existence, which is free from judgment.

In his description of mindfulness meditation, the spiritual teacher Sri Nisargadatta Maharaj wrote: *"Stop attributing names and shapes to the essentially nameless and formless, realize that every mode of perception is subjective, that what is seen or heard, touched or smelt, felt or thought, expected or imagined, is in the mind and not in reality and you will experience peace and freedom from fear."* Western teachers of mindfulness often use Massachusetts Medical School Professor Jon Kabat-Zinn's definition: *"Mindfulness means paying attention in a particular way; on purpose, in the present moment and non-judgmentally."*

Mindfulness is not limited to closed-eye meditative states. Our goal is to learn to be mindful at all times. Harvard psychologist Ellen Langer describes mindfulness as *"relinquishing preconceived mindsets and then acting on the new observations."* Looking at familiar objects and circumstances as if you've never seen them before is called *"Beginner's Mind,"* about which Zen master Shunry Suzuki proclaimed, *"In the beginner's mind there are many possibilities, but in the expert's there are few."*

The Buddhist monk, Thich Nhat Hanh, often speaks about walking mindfully. *"Walk as if you are kissing the Earth with your feet. ... Considering the act of each step we take as an infinite wonder and a joy will open our hearts like a flower, enabling us to enter the world of reality."*

Thay, as his students call him, also encourages mindful eating. *"When we pick up a piece of a vegetable, we look at it for half a second. We look mindfully to really recognize the piece of food, the piece of carrot or string bean. ... When we put it into our mouth, we know what we are putting into our mouth. ... Some of us, while looking at a piece of carrot, can see the whole cosmos in it, can see the sunshine in it, can see the earth in it. It has come from the whole cosmos for our nourishment. ... And when you chew, chew only the carrot, not your projects or your ideas. You are capable of living in the present moment, in the here and the now. It is simple, but you need some training to just enjoy the piece of carrot. This is a miracle."*

Introduction to Mindfulness Meditation

Stress management is preventive maintenance for people. Reducing stress supports good physical health as it expands mindful self-awareness. Instead of reacting reflexively to high anxiety and stress, there is wisdom in starting each day with a preemptive practice of how it feels to be safe, relaxed and self-aware.

The intention of stress reduction is to reassure the limbic brain it is safe, much as you would comfort a young child after a nightmare. As a formal practice, there are three basic steps to feeling safe and relaxed.

1. Close your eyes,
2. Breathe slowly,
3. Release muscular tension.

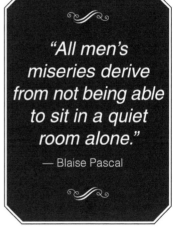

Begin by sitting in a comfortable position. Close your eyes and inhale slowly and deeply through your nose. Do this for three or four deep breaths before allowing your breathing to return to its natural rhythm.

"All men's miseries derive from not being able to sit in a quiet room alone."

— Blaise Pascal

As you exhale, create and sense the release of muscular tension and emotional anxiety throughout your body. Feel yourself softening like butter on a warm day, or imagine floating on a pool of water when its surface is as smooth as glass.

Then, gently focus your attention on the bottom of your nose, watching the natural ebb and flow of your body breathing itself. Recognize that you are not the breather, but rather the witness, observing gentle currents of air flowing smoothly, in and out, over the rim of your nostrils.

Do not admonish yourself when you realize your mind has drifted. Simply acknowledge the distraction, observing it just long enough to recognize its insignificance. Then, without frustration or self-recrimination, gently return your awareness to watching your breath at the bottom of your nose.

Practice this exercise for 10 to 20 minutes each day — ideally, in the morning. If you wish, visit the restroom and drink a small glass of water, but meditate before eating breakfast or consuming caffeinated drinks.

Mindfulness and Relaxation Research

Scientific research has repeatedly and verifiably shown meditation improves creative and abstract thinking as well as logic, imagination, insight, intuition, emotional sensitivity, memory, peak performance, conceptual understanding and overall self-awareness. In fact, there is evidence that mindfulness meditation generates physical growth in mature human brains, not only in neurons and capillaries but also in the thickness of the brain's predominant grey and white matter.

In 2006, psychologist Sara Lazar of the Harvard Medical School conducted one of the first studies to confirm brain growth in meditators. *"Our data suggest that meditation practice can promote cortical plasticity in adults in areas important for cognitive and emotional processing and well-being,"* Lazar reported. *"These increases are proportional to the time a person has been meditating during their lives ... and suggests that the thickness differences are acquired through extensive practice and not simply due to differences between meditators and non-meditators."*[23]

Three years later, Eileen Luders, postdoctoral research fellow at UCLA's Laboratory of Neuro-Imaging, used high-resolution 3-D MRIs to discover *"significantly larger cerebral measurements in meditators compared with controls, including larger volumes of the right hippocampus and increased grey matter in the right orbito-frontal cortex, the right thalamus and the left inferior temporal lobe. There were no regions where controls had significantly larger volumes or more grey matter than meditators."*[24] Because these areas of the brain are linked to emotion, Luders added: *"These might be the neuronal underpinnings that give meditators the outstanding ability to regulate their emotions and allow for well-adjusted responses to whatever life throws their way."*[25]

And in 2014, science writer Tom Ireland reported in the *Scientific American* blog: *"MRI scans show that after an eight-week course of mindfulness practice, the brain's fight or flight center, the amygdala, appears to shrink ... (and) the pre-frontal cortex — associated with higher order brain functions such as awareness, concentration and decision-making — becomes thicker. The functional connectivity between these regions – i.e. how often they are activated together – also changes. The connection between the amygdala and the rest of the brain gets weaker, while the connections between areas associated with attention and concentration get stronger."* [26]

The lesson is clear: relaxation (stress reduction) promotes awareness, emotional intelligence, understanding and wisdom. So, in this sense, wisdom can be learned through relaxation and mindfulness skills.

Vicious Cycles and Upward Spirals

Not only does ignorance stimulate fear, but inversely, fear promotes ignorance, confusion and unawareness. Fearing the unknown is a dynamic process that feeds upon itself — a vicious cycle of tension that pulls us deeper and deeper into a paralyzing stupor of painful emotions.

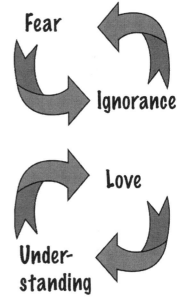

Relaxation and peaceful, loving feelings reverse that hurtful cycle to an upward spiral of insight and understanding, which helps us become safer and more relaxed. This positive cycle reveals love as wisdom — peace and harmony lifting us to levels of higher consciousness and expanded awareness.

We need to practice two concepts to shift from vicious cycles of fear and ignorance to upward spirals of love and understanding. The first is stress management — learning to release muscular tension and relax. The second is personal responsibility — recognizing our emotions as personal responses to ever-changing situations.

Victims portray themselves as effects of life, resisting and struggling against the flow of circumstances and events. They use fear as their shield and blame as their sword — a defensive, reflexive behavior that debilitates self-awareness.

Fearless Intelligence reveals the benefits of being accountable for our *responses* to fear and negativity. On the path of unfolding wisdom, we brandish love as our shield and truth as our sword to initiate behavior for the greater good of all.

In naming the design division of his company, Walt Disney borrowed the term *"imagineering"* from Alcoa Aluminum. He was fond of saying, *"If you can dream it, you can do it"* — a phrase that came to be known throughout Hollywood as *Disney Magic*.

Often we are so busy and stressed from reacting to life's problems, we forget our ability to conceive and act upon our imagination. Not only can we make our dreams come true, we can consciously initiate even-tempered, well-reasoned responses instead of reflexive reactions.

In his classic book, *Man's Search for Meaning*, Austrian psychiatrist Viktor Frankl writes, *"Between stimulus and response there is a space. In that space is our power to choose our response. In our response lies our growth and our freedom."* But as stress expands, the space between stimulus and response shrinks. Conversely, relaxation widens that interval, allowing us to choose appropriate responses.

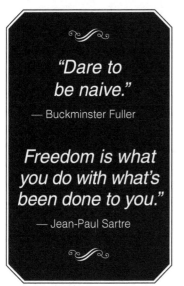

"Dare to
be naive."

— Buckminster Fuller

Freedom is what
you do with what's
been done to you."

— Jean-Paul Sartre

We've all heard the idiom, *"Life is what you make it,"* but few people believe it. Success guru Brian Tracy says only 3% of us have written goals, and less than 1% ever review them. Instead, most people nervously fixate upon the parts of life that appear to be done to them.

From time to time, everyone can be caught off-guard and victimized. But life is a two-way street — stimulus *and* response — and the parts that come from us are far more important than whatever seems to have been done to us. The author, Charles R. Swindoll wrote, *"Life is 10% what happens to you and 90% how you react to it."* John Lennon knew both sides of this, writing, *"Life is what happens to you while you're busy making other plans,"* as well as, *"Reality leaves a lot to the imagination."* Both are true.

Ten Keys to Mindfulness

1. ***Be Awake***. Meditation is the practice of awakening. Be aware of the way your thoughts filter and distort reality. Watch your trains-of-

thought without getting on-board. Every moment we spend multi-tasking, reviewing the past or worrying about the future is a moment that is lost forever. Awakening occurs in layers and levels. Practice, practice, practice.

2. ***Learn from Desire***. We can reject urges, cravings and desires once we recognize their subtle appeal. Notice the pull of procrastination, unhealthful food, the exaggerated need to check email, social media and TV. Material impermanence includes desires. They will come and go. We need not react.

3. ***Accept People and Things***. Acceptance is not the end of things, but the beginning. We must accept reality to change it. Accept failure and falling short as opportunities to learn. Accept the inevitability of distractions, and notice how quickly they lose their power to disturb you. Accept the uniqueness of others though they may frustrate and upset us. Accept the impermanence of life by treasuring the present moment. Accepting reality is not submitting or conceding, but simply acknowledging what is true in this moment.

4. ***Accept Discomfort***. When we resist pain, we hold on to it. To release pain, we must, first, let it in, and feel it to heal it. Unmanaged fear reflexively holds on to pain, bad habits, and dysfunctional relationships, as if the hurt is holding on to us. The Vietnamese Zen monk, Thich Nhat Hanh says, *"People have a hard time letting go of their suffering, out of a fear of the unknown, they prefer suffering that is familiar."* Instead, accept and let go.

5. ***Let Go of Expectations***. Watch your neediness and expectations in every situation — new projects, relationships and business deals. Drop judgment and your need for approval. The Second Noble Truth is: Desire, craving and attachment is the cause of all suffering.

6. ***Let Go of Illusions of Control***. We deceive ourselves by thinking we control things. Occasionally we can persuade or influence, but in truth, we have little or no control over what happens to us. By remaining balanced and flexile, we can manage our perception and response. Expect the unexpected.

7. **Watch Your Resistance**. The reality of impermanence guarantees a constant need to change and adapt, which in turn promotes stress. Observe your innate resistance to change, distraction, pain and everything else that annoys you. Impermanence is not the problem. Resistance is the problem. Watch it, and it will fade away.

8. **Be Curious**. We often get stuck in believing we know how things should be, including how people should behave. Instead, be curious. Let go of what you think you know, and explore what you do not know. Allow the joy of curiosity and understanding to replace the fear behind needing to be right.

9. **Be Grateful.** Gratitude is virtuous in the value it places on others. Besides being thankful, appreciation also means to grow. Gratitude attracts goodness and loving-kindness. Find reasons to be grateful for all experience without separating good from bad.

10. **Be Compassionate**. As you practice self-observation, you will become more empathetic. Empathy without judgment expands awareness, understanding and wisdom. This is the meaning of *"love your enemies"* and *"resist not evil."* Compassion and forgiveness are miraculous gifts to yourself.

Exercises:

Consider something you *know*, but don't *understand* very well. For example, you're familiar with the effects of gravity, and expect apples will fall from the tree. You may also know about Newton's Laws of Motion. But can you explain *how* gravity works? Do you really understand it?

Then reflect upon something about yourself that you know is true, but do not understand. Ask yourself why certain things upset you. Why do you feel disappointed when your expectations are not met? List a few things you strongly care about, and then consider why you care so much.

CHAPTER 5 —
WHAT IS LOVE?

Not only do you have the love you're looking for,
you are the love you're looking for.

My wife, Doreen, and I moved from Los Angeles to the Hawaiian Island of Maui in 2007 to produce a series of personal development audio programs called *Finding Your Self in Paradise.* We had planned a two-year project, but we stayed five years until the allure of family and friends brought us back to L.A.

Maui is a relatively small island, 48 miles long and 26 miles across at its widest point. The residential population is about 120,000 people, though over 2.2-million tourists visit each year. The northeastern or windward side receives over 300 inches of rain annually. Yet the average rainfall on the leeward south and west coasts, best known to tourists, is about 13 inches per year. With residents living as high as 4,000 feet on the 10,023-foot Haleakala Volcano, countless microclimates offer a variety of living experiences. We lived in Maui's rural Upcountry region — Makawao and Kula — amid cattle ranches, farms and residents of every imaginable ethnicity.

The volcanic vent that forms the archipelago comes out of the Pacific's mid-ocean ridge, making Hawaii the world's most remote islands. Consequently, the plants and animals have evolved in isolation. Many are endangered and unique to Hawaii. The Polynesian people first settled the islands between 300 and 500 CE (AD). A second, larger immigration followed between 1,000 and 1,300 CE.

Once British explorer Captain James Cook arrived in 1778, the culture was changed forevermore. As reports of this tropical paradise reached Europe and America, missionaries, whalers and land speculators descended on the remote island chain. Besides bringing the first rats and roaches to the Hawaiian Kingdom, Haoles (foreigners, usually Caucasian) also introduced smallpox, whooping cough, measles, influenza, dysentery and the common cold. Having no prior exposure and therefore no immunity to these strange diseases, hundreds of thousands of Hawaiians died.

Despite some degree of understandable hostility toward their Haoli occupiers, Hawaiians have remained a hospitable and compassionate people. Their acceptance of Aloha as a life force is mystical, panentheistic and not unlike the perennial philosophies of Vedantism, Buddhism, Taoism, Sufism, Neo-Platonism and Theosophy. The Aloha Spirit of the Polynesian culture in Hawaii is even more beautiful than its tropical flowers, luminous rainbows, lush rain forests, towering waterfalls and multicolored beaches.

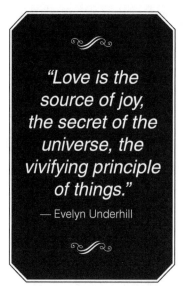

"Love is the source of joy, the secret of the universe, the vivifying principle of things."

— Evelyn Underhill

Tragically, self-righteous Christian missionaries destroyed their holy heiaus (temples) and slandered their kahuna (priests) as devil-worshippers. By 1819, their ancient religious practices were outlawed. The Hawaiian language, sacred hulas and chants were nearly lost. Fortunately, a nationalistic movement in the 1870s, and a revival of Hawaiian music in the 1970s ensured the survival of the island's Polynesian culture.

Encouraged by the gentle weather to live outdoors year-round, Hawaiians delight in the harmony of Nature. They revere kindness, equanimity, peace and love — not only emotional love, but the refined, unconditional Spiritual Love that is Aloha.

Taken literally, Alo-ha means *"the breath of God."* It is absolute love and acceptance. Therefore, all things are sacred — the volcano, the plants and animals, the ocean and fish, the sky and birds, the sun, moon and stars. Everything lives and breathes. Though separate in appearance, the wise Hawaiian kahuna are fond of saying, *"all come from the same rainbow (ānuenue)."*

The primary ideals of this mystical culture are imbued with Love, including:

- **Mana** — the Divine Life Force flowing through and connecting all things.

- **Aumakua** — a mortal human's overshadowing soul, spiritual essence or ancestral spirit.

- **Aina** — the land as a diverse but unified ecosystem, supporting all life with food, water and air. Hawaiians love the Aina as uniformly sacred from caldera to ocean floor, feeding the people and engendering their children.

- **Ohana** — the extended family plus close friends and neighbors; the basic unit of Hawaiian culture.

- **Pono** — righteousness, doing the right thing for the greatest good of all.

- **Kuleana** — your personal accountability and responsibility to help other people.

- **Mele** — a traditional chant or song to numerous deities, celebrating the love of Life and Nature. Music includes sacred hula dancing accompanied by slack-key guitar, slide guitar, ukulele, three-stringed ukeke (jaw harp), the xaphoon (bamboo saxophone), nose flute, conch shell and three basic percussion instruments — the pahu drum, the ipu (a large rattle made from gourds) and the ka'eke'eke (a bamboo slapstick).

The Greatest of All Mysteries

Just as a novel tells us about its author and a painting reflects the artist, the universe disclosures the Creative Life Force in all things. That Life Force has many names, chief among them Love, Consciousness, Wisdom and Awareness. Beyond the emotional feelings associated with Love, we find the ultimate Awareness — the inclusivity of the Universe, one thing *(uni)*, turning around *(verse)*.

The primary creed in all philosophy and theology is the understanding that *'everything is Love, and therefore, Absolute and Sacred.'* Further, non-dual philosophies insist that even wickedness and corruption are a necessary polarity of the One Thing.

"Love is the energy from which all people and things are made. You are connected to everything in your world through love."
— Dr. Brian L. Weiss, psychiatrist and hypnotherapist

"We search for love outside ourselves when love is all around us. Love is everywhere."
— Don Miguel Ruiz, shaman

"The kingdom is inside of you, and it is outside of you."
— Jesus Christ, Gospel of Thomas (3)

"Love is a force that connects us to every strand of the universe."
— Emily Hilburn Sell, author

"If you love everything, you will perceive the divine mystery in things."
— Fyodor Dostoevsky, author

"Love is the only thing that's real. Everything else is an illusion."
— Marianne Williamson, author

"That Love is all there is, Is all we know of Love."
— Emily Dickinson, poet

"Be drunk with Love, for Love is all that exists."
— Jalál ad-Dín Muhammad Rúmí, Sufi saint

"The eye through which I see God is the same eye through which God sees me; my eye and God's eye are one eye, one seeing, one knowing, one Love."
— Meister Eckhart, philosopher and mystic

Not only do we already *have* the love we're looking for, we *are* the Love we're looking for. Because everything is sacred, a resolute intention to love without judgment, to love even our enemies with compassion and forgiveness redeems all fear, heartache and confusion.

We will never understand Love as long as we think of it only in emotional terms. In its fullness, Love is Awareness, the miracle of sentience that endows us with perception and comprehension. It is the celestial conscience that imbues us with logic, imagination, intuition, empathy and a wide range of physical and emotional sensations, from excruciating torment to ineffable joy.

As Awareness, Love is the driving force and vivifying principle of Life. It is *fearless intelligence*, freedom and serenity. Love is the formless magnetic power upon which all form takes shape, lives, moves and has Its Being. Love is the Way, the Light and the Path by which we seek goodness, truth and beauty. In an impermanent and ever-changing universe, Love alone remains fully inclusive, eternal and infinite.

Love is the ultimate reality — the definitive Truth. It alone creates order out of chaos, redeems the imperfect and harmonizes multiplicity into Oneness. Love is Absolute, the Ground of Being, the Godhead of All That Is.

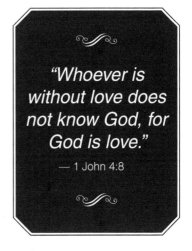

"Whoever is without love does not know God, for God is love."

— 1 John 4:8

Alchemical Gold

In their search for a means of transmuting one elemental metal into another, medieval alchemists learned to extract gold from ore with superheated ovens called athanors. Over time, the fires of the athanor burned away the ore's dross until only gold remained. These metaphorically minded Hermetic scientists thought the scorching adversity of life might burn off humanity's evil nature until only Divine qualities remain.

As this spiritual allusion of purgation became better known, the athanor was called the *Philosopher's Furnace*. Representing purification and the responsibility of power, the athanor's blazing flames were dubbed the *Philosopher's Sword*, while the term *Philosopher's Stone* symbolized the crystallization of knowledge and reason into enlightened moral wisdom. In this way, the mythical Arthurian *sword in the stone* was not a test of physical strength, but a wizard's assay to disclose the moral purity and spiritual worthiness of contenders for Camelot's throne.

Despite the alacrity with which humans can kill, torture, rape, slander and steal, our capacity for love, respect, forgiveness and compassion stands in sharp contrast. And though the fear of anything unknown appears to suppress human goodness, Love is the gold that survives the purgation of man's impurities.

Fear is an abyss of unawareness and ignorance. Love is the substantial quality of awareness and wisdom — radiant, cohesive, redemptive, eternal and infinite. Russian author Leo Tolstoy wrote, *"Seize the moments of happiness, love and be loved! That is the only reality in the world, all else is folly."* More recently, John Lennon sang, *"Love is real. Real is love."*

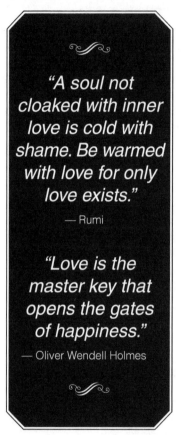

"A soul not cloaked with inner love is cold with shame. Be warmed with love for only love exists."

— Rumi

"Love is the master key that opens the gates of happiness."

— Oliver Wendell Holmes

The noblest *purpose* of human evolution is the personal growth that comes from our willingness to redeem ignorance and fear with understanding and love. The *meaning* of life is found in how we pursue our passions and interests.

Psychologist Erich Fromm wrote, *"There is no meaning to life except the meaning man gives his life by the unfolding of his powers."* Writer Hermann Hesse agreed. *"We insist life must have a meaning — but it can have no more meaning than we ourselves are able to give it. Because individuals can do this only imperfectly, religions and philosophers have tried to supply a comforting answer to the question. The answers all amount to the same thing: love alone can give life meaning. In other words: the more capable we are of loving and of giving ourselves, the more meaning there will be in our lives."*

Love is the yellow brick road, the only safe passage through the uncertainty, insecurity and impermanence of life. It is the spiral path to our Infinite Source. There is no path to love, for Love is *the Way* — just as there is no way to peace, because peace is the Way. And no way to happiness, as happiness is the Way.

Love, peace and happiness live eternally as the Awareness of the indwelling soul. As the Persian poet Rumi has written, *"Your task is not to seek for love, but merely to seek and find all the barriers within yourself that you have built against it."*

Magnetic Love Flows One Way

There is only one Source of Love — Awareness, the Divine Absolute. Just as our emotional feelings are internal responses to external relationships, events and circumstances, the only love you'll ever feel is the Loving Awareness that enlivens each one of us.

When a puppy excitedly licks your face, the loving joy that lives within you is stimulated. But that love did not come from the puppy. Similarly, when someone compliments you or says they love you, the feeling that results is *your love*. The puppy and the person have encouraged you to feel safe enough to temporarily release your resistance to the Loving Life Force within.

Not only do our emotions come from within, rather than toward us from others, the Life Force (Loving Awareness) moves through us and out into the world. Perhaps the most shocking statement you'll read in this book is, *"You cannot get love from others. You can only give it away through kindness. The love you feel has always been and will always be within you."*

True love needs nothing in return — not love in kind, not even appreciation. By freely offering love, we enhance the flow through us. Like opening a water faucet, reducing the resistance boosts the flow.

Love is not a commodity that can be held or possessed. And it is much more than an emotional feeling. Love is Awareness — an energy that radiates a magnetic field, sometimes called an aura or etheric body. The feeling of two people sharing their love for each other comes from these force fields engaging, interacting and reinforcing each other.

It is understandable that we may believe each of us is exchanging love with others, but more accurately, our mutual attraction is like two magnets. When juxtaposed, the radiant force field of each magnet attracts it toward the other.

Others may stimulate the emotional and spiritual love we feel from our relationships, but the love is always within us. Only our fearful resistance limits the love we feel as we interact. When someone insults us, we're likely to tighten and unconsciously restrict the vital energies flowing through us. When someone is kind and loving, we relax, which enhances the flow. But the love we're looking for is always within us.

Love as Higher Consciousness

Another term for Loving Awareness is Higher Consciousness. It is the majesty of reality as goodness, truth and beauty — moment to moment without judgment. Sadly, most of us rarely glimpse the entirety of reality because our perception is filtered and distorted by our thoughts, beliefs, expectations, moods and attitudes.

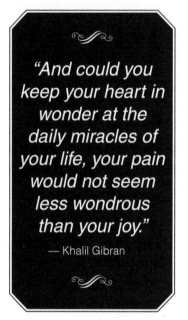

"And could you keep your heart in wonder at the daily miracles of your life, your pain would not seem less wondrous than your joy."

— Khalil Gibran

For example, take a moment right now to visualize a beautiful nature scene. Imagine how safe and relaxed you feel relishing the splendor all around you. Suddenly, a dangerous animal emerges — a tiger, a bear or a poisonous snake. The environment around you remains just as lovely, but your awareness is involuntarily altered by the apparent danger.

Self-awareness is restricted by mundane stress and anxiety in the same way, if not to the same degree. Our habitual attitudes and belief systems, desires and attachments inhibit and distort our awareness of the beauty, peace, freedom and joy that Reality constantly offers.

Though our enduring mental activity influences self-awareness, thinking is not vital to living. We do not faint or fall asleep when our mind *"goes blank"* for a moment or two — like suddenly forgetting what we're saying or whether we locked the door when we left home.

The initial sensory deprivation experiments in the mid-1950s surprised scientists who expected subjects would fall asleep when physical stimuli was blocked. Those who were somewhat sleepy often did fall asleep. But most subjects entered states of expanded awareness, often reporting profound insights and euphoric states of reverie.[27]

Self-awareness is not an effect of thinking. You cannot reason yourself into being more aware. On the contrary, thoughts distract us from the fullest awareness of our unfolding existence. The development of self-awareness requires us to consciously detach and step back or rise above our mental commotion — to watch and witness our mental and emotional reactions before choosing whether to agree or take part.

Don't Believe Everything You Think

Who are you when your thoughts clash? Our thought patterns and belief systems are often false and misleading, and logic can deceive us. Just because all crows are black does not mean all black birds are crows.

We are much more than *the thinker*. We have the ability to pause and reflect upon our thoughts before assuming they are reliable. Refusing to accept every thought as valid reveals our identity as self-awareness — able to consciously choose a response; or perhaps, to not respond at all. Detaching awareness from thought and feeling engenders wisdom.

Self-aware individuals refuse to become victims of their feelings and thoughts. Accepting accountability for our actions and reactions is not self-blame, but self-empowerment. Choosing to be happy for no particular reason, while learning from our heartache and frustration, is liberating.

Self-awareness allows us to sidestep high anxiety and confusion by remembering our choices —more options than are immediately apparent. Just as we can switch from deliberate breathing to watching our body reflexively breathe itself, we can switch from rote thinking to a non-judgmental awareness of thoughts unfolding on their own.

The Fear of Our Shadow Self

Few things are as frightening as exploring the truth of our authentic individuality. The separated self — the personality or ego we presume our self to be — is a role we play. The Latin word *persona* refers to the theatrical masks worn by ancient Greek and Roman actors.

The awareness that there is goodness and depravity in every individual helps us appreciate the complexity, ambiguity and contradictions in those we encounter in daily living. Yet even when we accept the sweeping potential in each of us, we can be drawn into bifurcating the world into groups that are either wholeheartedly good or entirely bad.

The famous psychoanalyst Carl Jung viewed the human persona as having two parts — a civilized, ethical side and a demonic *"shadow self."* Perhaps Jung was inspired by Robert Louis Stevenson's novella, *"The Strange Case of Dr. Jekyll and Mr. Hyde."* A case can also be made that the current popularity of vampire and zombie stories reflects humanity's unconscious shadow side, while our obsession with superheroes reveals our deep-seated desire for a messiah or savior to deliver us from evil.

Ouroboros

Lemniscate

Given to searching for deep, symbolic meaning, Jung suggested humanity's shadow side is *"the invisible saurian tail that man still drags behind him. Carefully amputated, it becomes the healing serpent of the mysteries."*[28] This is a reference to the ancient Egyptian Ouroboros and Lemniscate, in which snakes shed their skin (ecdysis), representing the cycle of life, healing, reincarnation and spiritual immortality.

Though the shadow side is fear-based and survival-oriented, it provides the contrast needed to elevate and redeem our self-view. In Jung's words, *"Once one has experienced a few times what it is like to stand judgingly between the opposites, one begins to understand what is meant by the self. Anyone who perceives his shadow and his light simultaneously sees himself from two sides and thus gets in the middle."*[29]

There can be no light without shadow; no redemption without sin. To be illumined by love and compassion, we must confront our unconscious fear and ignorance. Only by standing between and above our egoic shadow and ethical conscience will we realize our authenticity and aspire to the refinement of our potential.

The shadow's unrelenting fear conforms to several conflicting themes. We are afraid of being alone, yet frightened by committed, loving relationships.

We are afraid of change, yet just as frightened by feeling stuck. We want to understand, but often feel as if ignorance is bliss. The more frightened we are, the more conservative and reactionary our social and political views become. For the most part, pro-war, pro-capital punishment, bigotry, misogyny, anti-union, anti-science and anti-intellectual hostility are reflections of unconscious personal fear.

While there is no end to the reasons nationalists and alt-right conservatives offer to explain their social and political views, research at New York University in 2017 reveals a biological predisposition linked to the volume of the amygdala — the limbic brain's primitive fight-or-flight center. Those with larger amygdalas tend to hold reactionary and conservative views. Subjects with a smaller fear center in their brain are more likely to be active in socially progressive causes and protests.[30]

Love as Spiritual Life Force

Life is cyclic. Nothing rests. Nothing lasts. Everything has its ebb and flow in a state of perpetual flux. So it's realistic to hope for improvement whenever we're unhappy or frightened.

> *"All the world's a stage, and all the men and women merely players: they have their exits and their entrances."*
>
> — William Shakespeare

Yet our enjoyment of life and desire for stability tempts us to overlook the basic Law of Impermanence *(anicca, anitya)*. It is foolhardy to presume our material possessions may never wear out, rust, rot or fade away, or believe the satisfaction of acquisition and possession should also persist.

Even emotional love produces both pleasure and pain. We cannot fully appreciate love, happiness or contentment as long as we ignore the truth of change and impermanence. We are naïve if we expect joy and fulfillment without heartache and loss. Only Spiritual Love as Supreme Awareness is unconditional and eternal.

Before initiating change, we must first accept the reality of what's happening right now, before our very eyes. By even labeling circumstances as right or wrong, good or bad, happy or sad, we are filtering and distorting the peace, joy and contentment each moment guarantees if only we can learn to accept the truth of things exactly as they are.

Be clear about acceptance as a *beginning* rather than an end of things. Acceptance is not a synonym for helplessness. It's a reference to the need to acknowledge the truth of a present reality, especially if we intend to manage our response to it.

Love is non-judgmental Awareness — the acceptance and acknowledgment of what is authentically unfolding in the present moment. Love is Truth — the peak understanding of what is real and vital.

The pioneering psychiatrist Roberto Assagioli wrote, *"Deep in each one of us there is an inner pull toward some higher form of life, an underlying but insistent urge that prompts us — like the flower which innately turns toward the sun — to look toward something greater than ourselves."* Universal Love imbues the plants, flowers and trees with life. Not only do animals demonstrate loving care for their offspring, they often grieve the death of a companion. Love is everywhere. Even the mineral kingdom owes its cohesive strength to the vitality of this Life Force.

The Body of God

The word *spirit* originates in old French and Latin words meaning breath. Like electricity, spirit has both energy *(amperage)* and force *(voltage)*. Divine Will *(God's Mind, the Father)* is the energy of Spirit. Divine Love *(God's Heart, the Son)* is the magnetic force field. However, substantial manifestations of God's body, known as *theophany*, present a greater challenge.

The Christian New Testament says God does *not* have a body. In John 4:24, Christ says, *"God is Spirit."* And in Luke 24:39, Jesus told his disciples, *"… a spirit does not have flesh and bones as you see I have."*

Philosophers view the entire material universe and everything in it *(mater, the Mother)* as the embodiment of God, yet many religious people see no problem with visualizing the Creator in a human form. There are countless Biblical references to God as invisible. In Exodus 33:20, God tells Moses, *"But you cannot see my face, for man shall not see me and live."*

There are many other references in the Hebrew Bible (Old Testament), Greco-Roman pantheism and Eastern Vedantism of God the Father appearing in a physical human body. Hebrew theophanies include Abraham's claim that the God appeared to him in human form with two male angels at Mamre in the Hebron Valley. Abraham invited them to stay for dinner. (Genesis 18:8)

Also in Genesis (32:22-30), Jacob wrestles with a stranger who passes by late one evening. Eventually, the man cries out to Jacob, *"Let me go, for it is daybreak."* He then admits, *"You have struggled with God and with men and have overcome."* Jacob later says, *"I saw God face to face and yet my life was spared."* More commonly, God's disembodied voice is heard coming from a dense storm, a pillar of cloud or a burning bush.

The fear of idolatry and blasphemy prevented Catholic artists from painting images of God the Father in human form until the Renaissance. The best-known example, of course, is Michelangelo's fresco rendered in 1512 on the ceiling of the Vatican's Sistine Chapel. In 1682, sculptor Artus Quellin II went further, carving a large marble statue of God the Father in human form.

> *"Shall I say of you that you worship the image of your God that you have in your mind, but not your God?"*
> — Margaret Landon

> *"If horses had gods, they would look like horses."*
> — Xenophanes

Conceiving the Godhead in the image of mankind creates other problems. The Book of Proverbs lists half a dozen things that God hates, and there are countless Biblical references to His Divine Anger. However, hatred and anger are signs of deep hurt and fear, qualities you would not expect from God the Absolute.

A growing number of disaffected Christians find such idolatry degrading and puerile. Opinion polls show 37% of American adults now describe themselves as *"spiritual, but not religious."* Nearly three-quarters of the people who check *"None"* when asked to select their religion say they believe in God as a Universal Spirit.[31]

The main problem with portraying the Godhead as a remote and independent Being is the consequential sense that God has abandoned us. All but the most self-aware individuals often feel alienated and alone, condemned to live in shameful, naked bodies on a strange planet of separated and tenuous forms.

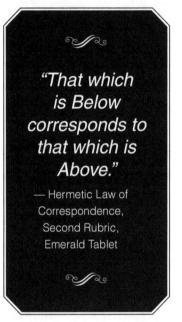

"That which is Below corresponds to that which is Above."

— Hermetic Law of Correspondence, Second Rubric, Emerald Tablet

We are taught to petition God with prayer, but not to listen for answers. We're told answers are only found in holy books, written thousands of years ago by men who believed the sun revolved around a flat Earth at the center of the Universe; and the stars were holes in the sky-dome where the radiance of heaven shone through.[32]

It's understandable that our ancient ancestors would personify Divinity as a distant human form. But everyone is now familiar with the invisible, magnetic emanations of radio and TV waves. So we're much more likely to recognize the Spiritual Source of things as a Universal Force Field of awareness, rather than a disconnected physical idol.

Mystical Love

The growing interest in spirituality free from religious dogma is essentially mystical because of its attraction to Divine Love as the congruent force field connecting All Things. The supposition that everything in the Universe is an inalienable extension, reflection or fragment of Divine Love has traditionally been called *pantheism.*

Religious fundamentalists spurn pantheism because it equates God with Nature. Pantheism views all material things as sacred, which means God expresses Itself as the vile snake as well as the noble eagle. God would be carnal and beastly as well as pure and perfect — fundamentally good, yet permitting the existence of evil.

Pantheists view evil as the *absence* of goodness and virtue, rather than a force that resists or opposes virtue. But an argument can be made that evil is a necessary contrast to goodness. Further, if Satan opposes God's purpose, why would hell be an inferno of eternal suffering? If the devil ruled hell independently, it would surely be a festival of depravity and wickedness rather than a netherworld of torture and punishment.

Panentheism expands upon *pantheism* by expressing Divinity as *both* immanent and transcendent. Immanent means God is in All Things. Transcendent signifies All Things existing within God, while acknowledging God to be unlimited, and therefore more than Its manifested Creation.

Just as the ocean is in every cloud and raindrop, God as Awareness must be present within all parts of Its Creation. Christ refers to the immanence of God in man when he says in Luke, *"Behold, the kingdom of God is within you."*[33] Jesus goes further in the Gnostic Gospel of Thomas, affirming both immanence and transcendence when he says, *"The king-dom is inside of you and it is outside of you."*[34]

"Love conquers all."

— Virgil

John quotes Jesus as saying, *"that all of them may be one, Father, just as you are in me and I am in you. May they also be in us so that the world may believe that you have sent me."*[35] And in the fifth book of the New Testament, Acts of the Apostles, Paul also describes God as ubiquitous Spirit rather than form, saying, *"For in Him we live and move and have our being."*[36] Mystical panentheists seek a personal connection to Divinity through Love and Awareness — the Life Force that imbues every scintilla of the physical creation and beyond.

While developing his theory of the *collective unconscious*, Dr. Carl Jung explored mystical ideas of God as a *relative* Truth as distinct from a spiritual *Absolute*. His notes include a passage that reads, *"The 'relativity of God,' as I understand it, denotes a point of view that does not conceive of God as 'absolute,' i.e., wholly 'cut off' from man and existing outside and beyond all human conditions, but as in a certain sense dependent on him. It also implies a reciprocal and essential relation between man and God, whereby man can be understood as a function of God, and God as a psychological function of man."* [37]

The Mysticism of Star Wars

Before writing his first *Star Wars* novel, George Lucas consulted mythologist Joseph Campbell about ancient metaphysical views of a universe suffused with a vital Life force, not unlike the monism of Hermetic Alchemy, Cabbala, Rosicrucianism, Neo-Platonism, Sufism, Vedantism, Buddhism and Taoism. In the first film, the Jedi Wizard Obi-Wan Kenobi describes the Force to young Luke Skywalker as *"an energy field created by all living things. It surrounds us and penetrates us; it binds the galaxy together."*

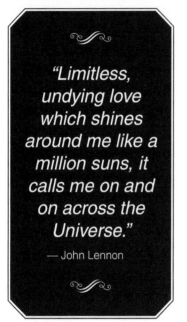

"Limitless, undying love which shines around me like a million suns, it calls me on and on across the Universe."

— John Lennon

In the second movie, Yoda further teaches Luke, *"My ally is the Force, and a powerful ally it is. Life creates it; makes it grow. Its energy surrounds and binds us. Luminous Beings are we, not this crude matter. You must feel the Force around you. Here ... between you, me, the tree, the rock, everywhere."*

The Force in Star Wars has an evil, *"dark side"* — arrogance, selfishness, hatred, envy, greed and anger. But the Jedi adage, *"May the Force be with you,"* refers to the good side — love, conscious awareness, wisdom, truth, beauty, kindness and compassion. As the film series progresses, we learn the dark side is ultimately the weaker of the two.

The Qualities of Spiritual Love

The qualities of Love are many. A partial list includes caring, kindness, ethical conduct, acceptance, compassion, fearlessness, trust, respect, selflessness, generosity, gratitude, non-attachment, healing, the longing for justice, appreciation of truth, beauty, humor, humility and patience.

As a Universal Force Field, Divine Love — also known as Spiritual Awareness, Consciousness and the Absolute — has several qualities similar to electromagnetic force fields and electricity. As energy, Love has force and resistance, frequency and polarity, inductance and capacitance, radiance and magnetism. Unlike electromagnetism, love is redemptive. It heals, transmutes and transforms as it grows, evolves, improves, refines and uplifts. It is the Way, the Path and the Salvation from the suffering of incarnation, transmigration, fear and mortality.

More than an emotional feeling, Love exists on many frequencies, from raw lust to romance, friendship and kinship, humility and kindness, forgiveness, compassion, generosity, gratitude, equanimity, tolerance, patience, humor, aesthetics, understanding and wisdom. Even the willingness to sacrifice your life for others is a phenomenon of Love.

Buddhist philosophy proposes four qualities of true love — joy, loving-kindness, equanimity and compassion. Yet each quality contains the other three in keeping with the non-dual view that separation of any kind is an illusion.

The ancient Greeks also recognized four types of love — storgé, philia, éros and agápe. The first three types are emotional. Storgé is affection, fondness or brotherly love, especially among family members. Philia is the bond of friendship. Éros is romance and includes sexual attraction, passion and intimacy.

Once known as Charity, agápe is unconditional Spiritual Love. Unfortunately, both words — agápe and Charity — are now archaic. When not capitalized, the word charity has come to mean financial assistance and goodwill. When capitalized, Charity formerly meant loving everyone absolutely and unconditionally, as God loves by causing *"His sun to rise on the evil and the good and sends rain on the righteous and the unrighteous."*[38]

As an omnipresent force field connecting Spirit and matter, Christian agápe and Charity are similar to the Spiritual Awareness of Eastern Vedantism. Although God and humanity are separate in Judeo-Christian and Islamic monotheism — virtual opposites following the fall from Eden — God and mankind commune remotely through the medium that is Agápe Love or Christ Consciousness.

In about 800 BCE, the spiritual Upanishads cultivated a non-dual actuality from the early Vedic philosophies. Sages realized that the appearance of separation is an illusion of the mind — that there are neither edges nor limitations to physical form; that all matter exists as fields of energy in a cohesive universe.

Om Symbol

The inclusivity of love as an omnipresent spirit is found in all spiritual teachings, even though religious practices are often limited by sectarian dogma. There is value in remembering that Buddha was not a Buddhist, Christ was not a Christian and Muhammad was not a Muslim. They were all teachers of Love as harmony, unity and awareness.

As Awareness, Spiritual Love connects, harmonizes and sustains all material forms into extensions or reflections of One Spiritual Essence (One Mind, One Heart). The Om symbol, revered in Hinduism, Buddhism, Sikhism and Jainism, represents non-dual monism (Panpsychism) unifying the Godhead, Brahman, with all things.

Though mystics recognize spiritual Love as inclusive, it has a particular affinity for organic life forms. Behind our basal metabolic rate, we are animated and illumined by Awareness, also called Love, Aetheric Light, Holy Spirit or Holy Ghost, Chi, Rei ki, Kundalini, Prana, Mana, Orenda, Ruach (*ruah ha-qodesh*), Baraka, pneuma, élan vital and more. It correlates to the Christos, the Divine Breath, the Buddha nature, Nirvana, Heaven and the Collective Soul of all beings. Love as Awareness is the Kingdom within.

Emotional Love and Fear

Emotional love is a subsidiary function of Spiritual Love — a lower correspondence, reflection or extension of Divinity. While Spiritual Love is unconditional, emotional love has its polarities — pleasure and heartache, fulfillment and desolation. When we become stressed or disturbed, our emotions swing from love into hurtful, fear-based feelings.

Spiritual Love induces many wonderful qualities of self-awareness into the mortal, incarnated self. However, fear carried as muscular tension, impedes Spiritual Love, leading to an entire range of hurtful, negative emotional feelings.

Most people find the fear of living more terrifying than the fear of dying and are more frightened of understanding themselves than of strangers. In her book *Return to Love* (1992), author Marianne Williamson wrote, *"Our deepest fear is not that we are inadequate. Our deepest fear is that we are powerful beyond measure. It is our light, not our darkness that most frightens us."*

Similarly, Toltec shaman Don Miguel Ruiz said, *"Our biggest fear is taking the risk to be alive and express what we really are."* The Swiss death and dying psychiatrist Elisabeth Kübler-Ross wrote, *"It is not the end of the physical body that should worry us. Rather our concern must be to live while we're alive — to release our inner selves from the spiritual death that comes with living behind a facade designed to conform to eternal definitions of who and what we are."*

Fear is a nightmare, an illusion — a signal indicating insufficient awareness and understanding. Like most emotion, fear is unreasonable. Little benefit comes from thinking about fear, anxiety or stress. It must be resolved by intuition rather than logic — emotional affect, not rational conclusion.

"There is no fear in love. But perfect love drives out fear."

— 1 John 4:18

The fear of being alone, called *separation anxiety* or autophobia, is common. Yet others fear love and intimacy — philophobia. Nyctophobia is fear of the dark, while heliophobia is a fear of sunlight.

The fear of being out of control runs through all phobias except for paralipophobia, which is the fear of being responsible and in-control. Phobophobia is the fear of fear itself and panphobia is the fear of everything. Where is the logic in any of this?

As the Source of all love, universal Spiritual Love ranks the happiness of others ahead of the ego's self-centered desires. Craving the attention and affection of others suggests a backward view of love. We don't need others to love us before we can love them. Remember that love does not come *to us from others*, but rather *through us to others*. As those we love reflect it back, it is amplified in a shared force field of love, kindness, humility and compassion.

Instead of needing others to love and care for us, we can give love without condition once we understand it as the primal Life Force coursing through us. Love continuously radiates, like the sun. Dark nights and cloudy skies may lead you to believe the sun has abandoned you. But be not deceived. We may lose the object of our love, but Love cannot be lost. Not even death can extinguish Love.

As long as we allow ourselves to be emotionally vulnerable and spiritually aware, we will be filled with love without reason. In the light of this abundance of self-love and self-awareness, we aspire only to radiate our love of life outward in all directions — to lovers, friends and enemies, too.

> *"The object of this love is not found outside self in societies of individuals, nor in the external world, but within self, in the divine self whose essence is that very love."*
>
> — Leo Tolstoy

The Rubber Life Raft Metaphor

Imagine two people adrift at sea in a rubber life raft. Neither can swim and they have no life preservers. One asks the other, *"What will we do if this raft springs a leak? We'd sink like rocks."*

They sit quietly, pondering their fate. Suddenly, one gets what appears to be a great idea and shouts out, *"Hey, since neither of us can swim, we'll just have to save each other! I'll rescue you; then you can save me."*

Obviously, this is an absurd idea. How can two non-swimmers save each other? Yet consider the behavior of lonely, empty people who visit online dating sites, bars and singles events looking for love from other lonely, empty people. In the initial flush of excitement when romantic chemistry does occur, each is thinking, *"I'll love them, if they love me."*

What kind of romance is this? We promise to fill each other's empty spots, as if, *"I have no love, and you have no love. So, we'll just love each other."* Really? And where will this love come from? Does that vow make any more sense than two non-swimmers promising to rescue each other if their life raft sinks?

The curious part of this fabled romance, however, is that for 30 to 90 days, it seems to work. Swept away by those wonderful, giddy feelings of love, we think of little else. We forget to eat and often can't sleep as unrestrained joy and happiness spills into all areas of life. Yet in time, the emptiness returns — for it is *our* emptiness. Temporarily, we were filled — not by another's love so much as by our own hope, expectation and willingness to release our fear.

Said simply, emotions are unique and personal responses. They are contagious; so other people, external events and circumstances can stimulate them. But nevertheless, emotional feelings are our internal reactions to outside stimuli. To claim that someone *"made me angry"* or even *"made me feel loved"* is misleading.

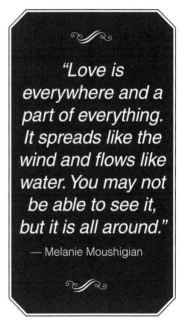

If 10 people are insulted by identical words, each will show somewhat dissimilar reactions. Our emotional responses reveal us, not the provocateur. Initially, we'll feel victimized, even after we've accepted responsibility for our emotions. So we must develop our self-awareness to reduce the time it takes to *own* a response. It's helpful to remember the famous Eleanor Roosevelt quote, *"No one can make you feel inferior without your consent."* More completely, no one can make you feel *anything* without your consent.

"Love is everywhere and a part of everything. It spreads like the wind and flows like water. You may not be able to see it, but it is all around."

— Melanie Moushigian

Strong, healthy relationships are built upon self-love — recognizing our capacity as conduits of Divinity to offer kindness, trust and respect to others without judgment. Spiritual self-love is humble as we receive it from Divine Abundance, then offer it to the world, needing nothing in return.

Egotistical self-love is not really love at all, but a pathetic clinging to our fears of being unlovable. To participate successfully in loving relationships, we must know what's lovable about us and what we have to offer others.

The Need to Be Loved

Being aware is more than being conscious. And being self-aware transcends being self-conscious. Consciousness means to be awake, alert and responsive, while awareness implies a meaningful understanding of our individuality, relationships and situations.

Self-aware refers to understanding our desires, motives and passion. However, self-conscious suggests an exaggerated concern about how other people may judge us as respectable, acceptable and lovable.

A few years ago, a client we'll call Nancy visited my personal development office in Los Angeles. The first thing anyone would have noticed about Nancy was her striking attire. She was dressed to impress — overdressed, really, in a vivid red gown topped by a luxurious fur wrap. Large diamond earrings and a garish necklace sparkled and rattled as she moved.

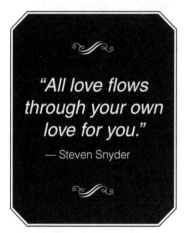

"All love flows through your own love for you."

— Steven Snyder

During our initial intake session, Nancy explained that she and her husband had recently won the California State Lottery — an especially large jackpot, she assured me. I congratulated her and cut to the chase.

"Having encountered such good fortune, how might I be able to help you?" I inquired.

"Well, my boss won't let me work for him anymore," she replied sadly. *"He thinks I should enjoy my wealth instead of coming to work every day."*

That made sense to me, so I asked Nancy, *"And this is a problem for you because …?"*

"Because I love going to work," she said.

Nancy spent the next few minutes explaining her job to me. She was an office manager for a small insurance company. Her skills included word processing, QuickBooks and basic office management.

"Well, if you like your job so much," I suggested, *"why don't you apply for a similar position with another company?"*

Obviously frustrated with me, Nancy squirmed in her seat. *"Because I like THAT job,"* she barked. She then began to tear up, and dabbing her eyes with a fine linen handkerchief, said softly, *"I love those people. I need them in my life."*

I explained to Nancy, *"Needy love is not healthy. It's childish and pushes people away. Believing there is love in needing to be loved is like expecting hunger to nourish you."*

Watching Nancy's face to gauge her receptivity, I added, *"You'd feel a lot better if we worked to turn this around and help you be more independent. Only when we give love will we feel truly loved. Feeling lovable and loving is up to you."*

Unfortunately, Nancy was hearing none of it. She was terrified by no longer being needed at work, which to her meant no longer being loved. In Nancy's mind, winning the lottery had made her unlovable. Like so many, she thought love came to her from others rather than through her.

Real love is unconditional. If we expect something in return, even gratitude, we're not presenting a gift, but instead, making a purchase. Love is like faith. It's easy to believe the Universe loves and supports us when things are going well. The question is whether our faith abides when circumstances appear to conspire against us. We are corresponding fragments of the One Life, and when we love everyone for no reason, happiness abounds for no reason.

Just as a dimmer switch reduces the brightness of a light bulb by increasing electrical resistance, fear and anxiety carried as physical tension diminish the Life Force we feel as love, happiness and contentment. Feeling safe and relaxed lowers resistance, boosting the Life Force flowing through us. This added vitality promotes emotional and physical healing, uplifts our moods, attitudes and energy levels and illumines our conscious awareness, insight and understanding.

Love Is Letting Go

Everyone wants more love and less fear. However, our fight-or-flight response triggers muscular tension — a feeling of holding on that resists the flow of love. Only when we feel safe enough to let go of tension will we again feel peaceful, loving, kind and compassionate. Whenever you feel stuck, consider that, instead, you're holding on to tension, heartache and false beliefs.

It may seem counter-intuitive to say fear is holding on and love is letting go, but watch people riding a roller coaster. Despite being securely strapped in, frightened riders hold on as tightly as possible. Those who love the excitement let go, raising their arms high above their heads, laughing and cheering.

Even though our reflexive tension leads us to hold on to fear, it often feels like the fear is holding on to us. Rather than resisting fear, we must acknowledge it and the hurt it causes. Only when we fully feel all of our heartache and anxiety, even the most frightening, can we understand and release it.

> "Usually we think that brave people have no fear. The truth is that they are intimate with fear."
> — Pema Chodron

The urge to *"love unconditionally"* requires unrestricted awareness, which means feeling *all of our emotions*, not just the positive ones. If we diminish our awareness to ignore or deny discomfort — whether emotional or physical pain — our brains will amplify it. In its place, the courage to allow all feelings to have their way with us, without condition — even if it feels like we're about to be crushed or devoured — will vanquish our distress, anguish and stinging tears.

The theosophical teacher, Jiddu Krishnamurti, wrote, *"What is needed, rather than running away or controlling or suppressing or any other resistance, is understanding fear; that means, watch it, learn about it, come directly into contact with it. We are to learn about fear, not how to escape from it."* Reread that Krishnamurti quotation, replacing the word *fear* with the word *pain* to see they are the same.

The Longing of the Part to Be Whole

Finally, consider that the ebb and flow of love in our lives may result from incarnation itself. Torn from the spiritual fabric of Divine Love, we are born alone into a material world of separated form. By all appearances, solid objects stand apart. Consequently, many people spend their entire lives trying to reconnect — searching, reaching out, desperately hoping the love of friends, family, pets or Nature will rekindle the Sacred Love experienced as Souls above and free of form.

In the 16th Century, Saint John of the Cross described his feelings of having been abandoned by God as his *"dark night of the soul."* More recently, the Italian psychiatrist Roberto Assagioli referred to his bouts of depression as *"divine homesickness."* This longing of the part to be whole is Love's magnetic nature pulling us toward our spiritual Source.

The Big Picture

Each one of us is an expression of Spiritual Love, the force of awareness. Love is the great *"I Am"* of the soul, eclipsing the egoic *me* and *mine*. As rivers flow and plants bloom, the human soul extends itself into physical form — material components of the Universal Life Force.

Though we are familiar with the instability of emotional love, its spiritual source is fixed and constant. The pendulum offers an apt analogy for the relationship between Spiritual Love and its emotional corollary. The fixed, unified pivot-point at the top of the pendulum represents the eternal and unconditional nature of Spiritual Love. The weighted bottom represents the mercurial energies of emotional love.

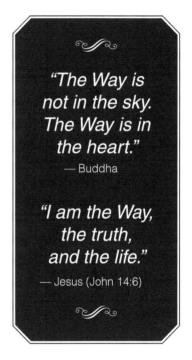

"The Way is not in the sky. The Way is in the heart."
— Buddha

"I am the Way, the truth, and the life."
— Jesus (John 14:6)

When we are contradicted, confused or unaware for any reason, fear and anxiety shift us out of alignment with our Spiritual Source. The hurtful and upsetting fear-based emotions that result alert us to the need for greater self-awareness. As we understand ourselves better, we return to our relaxed, safe and peaceful center and regain our loving, loved and lovable feelings.

The connection of emotional and Spiritual Love represented by the pendulum at rest has historically been called the *Way* in Christianity,

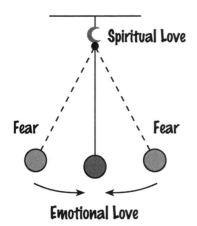

Spiritual Love

Fear   Fear

Emotional Love

Middle Way in Buddhism and the *Middle Pillar* in Freemasonry. Commonly symbolized by the spinal chakra system, the snake-wrapped caduceus, magic wand, king's scepter, wizard's staff and bishop's crosier, it is also known esoterically as the Path, Stairway to Heaven and Jacob's Ladder.[39]

Exercises:

Review the key points about Love in this chapter.

- Positive emotions — joy, happiness, contentment, equanimity, kindness, humility and generosity — are love-based. Stay the course.

- Negative emotions — sadness, disappointment, jealousy, frustration, anger, apprehension, embarrassment and shame — are fear-based. Make the changes needed to get back on course.

- Love and fear are **not** opposites like true or false, good or bad, winners or losers. They are complementary, like two sides of the same coin, a pair of gloves or the poles of a bar magnet. Also, they are not absolute, but relative since love often contains elements of heartache and fear.

Caduceus and Chakras

- Love is energy — like light and heat. Fear is the absence of energy — like darkness and cold.

- Fear cannot be overcome or conquered, but it can be released. Remember that anxious tension holds on to fear, even though we often feel as if the fear is holding on to us.

Magic Wand

Crosier

• Because Love is Divine and equally present everywhere, there's no need to hold on to it. Love is letting go of fear — the awareness and understanding that releases ignorance.

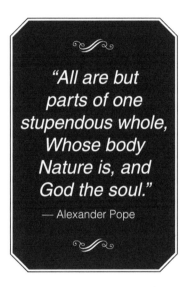

"All are but parts of one stupendous whole, Whose body Nature is, and God the soul."

— Alexander Pope

CHAPTER 6 —
LIVING MINDFULLY

Awareness unfolds as a holographic fractal. Everything is in the One, and the One is in every seemingly separate thing.

Doreen and I were winding our way through Beverly Hills and West Hollywood one afternoon when we decided a cup of strong coffee would perk us up. I suggested a Starbucks on the Sunset Strip that had easy parking, so we turned onto La Cienega Boulevard and headed up the hill.

The Sunset Strip is a perpetual carnival. New and intriguing sights demand attention. Besides the Venice Beach boardwalk, there's no better place in L.A. to people-watch. Day or night, the Strip is a trip.

As Doreen ordered coffee for both of us, I lingered at the pastry case. Against my better judgment, I surrendered to my cravings and bought an espresso brownie.

Eager to get home, we jumped back into the car and headed down the Strip chatting about the sights — giant electronic billboards, new shops and cafes, and the most wonderful assortment of people parading up and down the sidewalks.

At the end of the Strip, I turned left onto Crescent Heights to take Laurel Canyon into the San Fernando Valley. Reaching for the little bag with my espresso brownie in it, I was surprised to find only crumbs. Confused, I thought, *"Someone ate my brownie."*

I quickly concluded it wouldn't have been Doreen. She would have bought one for herself if she'd wanted it. And there was no dog in the car to blame.

Shifting my attention to my mouth and tongue, I sensed a faint hint of chocolate. I was stunned to realize I had unconsciously devoured the entire brownie, completely failing to savor its delectable sweetness.

But there was more. My disappointment turned to dismay as I wondered, *"What else have I missed? What if I find myself old and infirm before realizing my life is nearly over, and I forgot to pay attention?"*

It was a profound revelation. I knew about mindfulness. I had written and lectured about its significance for years. I had interviewed Jon Kabat-Zinn — one of the West's chief evangelists of living fully. Yet here I found myself a victim of my failure to remain mindfully aware.

> "The best way to capture moments is to pay attention. This is how we cultivate mindfulness. Mindfulness means being awake. It means knowing what you are doing.
>
> — Jon Kabat-Zinn

The brownie incident was a real awakening for me. The most important benefit of mindful awareness became crystal clear — my entire existence depends on it. Sometime later, I rediscovered Henry David Thoreau's most famous quotation, *"I went to the woods because I wished to live deliberately, to front only the essential facts of life, and see if I could not learn what it had to teach, and not, when I came to die, discover that I had not lived."*

Awareness Perceives Reality

Awareness is the essence of perception, comprehension and intelligence. It involves purposeful attention and self-observation, mindfully watching our emotions influence the unfolding of ideas. Most of our thoughts are not the result of deliberate reasoning. They are unstructured streams of confused, often irrational ideation that find their way into consciousness from the unconscious mind.

Being confused and lost in thought is unawareness. Arguably, my scrumptious brownie ceased to exist the moment I was no longer aware of it. Whenever we allow our self-awareness to drift from the present moment to past regrets, fears of the future or the distractions of multitasking, another portion of our unique and precious life is lost forever.

Some may say we are oblivious to our ignorance. Others might describe it as a fundamental dishonesty about how profoundly confused we are — or maybe it's just a lack of humility. In any event, ignorance indicates an absence of self-awareness more often than low intelligence.

Unfolding Self-awareness

Besides human beings, scientific researchers have discovered only nine other species of animals able to recognize themselves in a mirror. Four are primates — orangutans, chimpanzees, gorillas and rhesus monkeys; plus elephants, bottle-nosed dolphins, orca whales, ants and European magpies. Except for the magpie, all have brains with an outer layer called the cortex, which connects and coordinates various parts of the brain. Even though magpies and other crows have no cortex, they demonstrate exceptional intelligence and high self-awareness for reasons that remain a mystery.

> *"Mindfulness helps us freeze the frame so that we can become aware of our sensations and experiences as they are, without the distorting coloration of socially conditioned responses or habitual reactions."*
>
> — Henepola Gunaratana

Humans develop the ability to recognize their mirror image between 14 and 18 months of age, but the customary definition of self-awareness in human adults goes far beyond the mirror test. Self-aware people have knowledge of their own individuality — their thought patterns and belief systems, emotional feelings and moods, attitudes and motives. Self-awareness also facilitates empathy for others and a sense of how they may perceive us.

Dr. Philippe Rochat at Emory University's Department of Psychology has proposed a five-stage model of unfolding self-awareness.

Level 1: Differentiation — The sense of self as a separated being begins when infants recognize a distinction between their own bodily movements in a mirror and the movement of other people and things elsewhere in the world.

Level 2: Situation — In this stage, infants contemplate the separation between living within their own body and its external reflection in the mirror.

Level 3: Identification — Growing beyond their awareness of the mirrored image as separated from the world and the self, children now realize the mirror is reflecting an image of *"Me"* and no one else. Evolutionary psychologists view this as a significant stage of cognitive growth. Developmental psychologists describe it as the emergence of the conceptual self.[40]

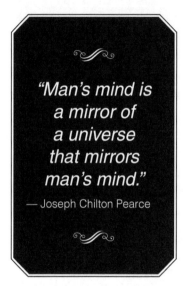

"Man's mind is
a mirror of
a universe
that mirrors
man's mind."

— Joseph Chilton Pearce

Level 4: Permanence — This is the stage at which children begin to understand their existence across space and time. Presented with still photos and videos, we recall the past and anticipate the future, spreading outside the Zen-like presence of here and now.

Level 5: Self-consciousness — Concern about how we appear to others is a level of maturity that most adults never surpass. Children who yell, *"Look at me; watch this,"* not only want attention and approval, but also seek to affirm their existence and impact on the world.

The Five Types of Awareness

As mature adults, we experience five basic types of conscious awareness. The most refined is meta-awareness (spiritual awareness or metacognition), which is *the awareness of being consciously aware*. The remaining four are mental, emotional and physical awareness, plus perception of external objects, situations and events.

The awareness of most people is consumed by stimuli from their physical environment and mental thought process. Conscious behavior is third, as most of our actions are habitual or reflexive. Fourth is our emotional nature. We remain unaware of most feelings unless or until they overwhelm us, though women tend to be more emotionally aware than men. Lastly, the awareness of being conscious is so arcane, most people never consider it.

The two least developed types of awareness — emotions and consciousness — can be the most fulfilling. Since repressed emotions can trigger impulsive, reactionary behavior, the equanimity in self-awareness is needed to produce a deliberately levelheaded, even-tempered approach to understanding. Further, the appeal of aesthetics, kindness, honesty, morality, justice, humor and wisdom relies on emotional rather than mental awareness. The beauty of a flower, a lilting melody or a sleeping baby is understood by feeling, not reasoning.

In the same way, we are not what we think of ourselves as much as we are what we love and care about. As stated in the previous chapter, *we are the love we seek*. Healthy self-love is typically concealed by fears of inadequacy and confusion about what other people may think of us.

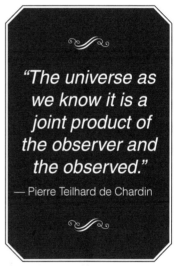

"The universe as we know it is a joint product of the observer and the observed."

— Pierre Teilhard de Chardin

Physical awareness includes behavioral, social and situational awareness. Improving behavioral awareness is mostly about replacing reflexive reactions with well-considered, purposeful alternatives. Social awareness includes empathy, kindness, leadership and motivational skills. Situational awareness recognizes external circumstances and anticipates potential hazards and the consequences of particular actions.

Strangely, only five percent of the known universe is palpable, meaning 95% of it exists beyond our senses. Between 23% and 27% of the universe is invisible *dark matter*. It does not emit or reflect light, cannot be touched or felt and is unaffected by electromagnetism. Scientists became aware of it only because of its gravitational effect on tangible matter. *Dark energy* makes up 68% to 72% of the universe. It became apparent after researchers discovered the universe is expanding at a constantly accelerating velocity.

Even within the conventional material world, humans cannot hear sounds pitched higher than 20 kilohertz, nor see frequencies of light below red or above violet. Our smelling and tasting senses are relatively undeveloped compared to many other animals. At our best, we are mentally aware of only the tiniest fraction of the reality in which we are immersed.

In a short essay in 1936, Albert Einstein drew upon the ancient Ethiopian proverb, *"Fish discover water last,"* writing, *"Of what is significant in one's own existence, one is hardly aware, and it certainly should not bother the other fellow. What does a fish know about the water in which he swims all his life?"* Also in the mid-to-late 1960s, communications theorist Dr. Marshall McLuhan was fond of telling his audiences, *"We don't know who discovered water, but we are pretty sure it wasn't a fish!"*

Everything that appears to exist outside us is conceived within, an awareness that supports the veracity of a non-dual reality. We observe the external world as reflected light strikes photoreceptor cells sending electrical impulses to our brain where they are organized and comprehended. And while our emotions may arise spontaneously from within, many are internal reactions to external stimuli.

Non-duality erases all distinctions between subject and object. The ancient Sanskrit word *advaita* translates to *not two* or *no second*. As a central principle of Vedantic philosophy, our ultimate existence as fields of energy (spirit) nullifies all notions of a separated physical self.

In other words, physical forms are illusions. As ice, water appears solid, and liquid water has a surface boundary. But as clouds, water vapor has no border or definable form. Because all matter is ultimately force fields of energy, all separation is merely an appearance.

Our fingers look separate and distinct until we recognize them as extensions of a single hand. Our hands and arms appear divergent until we notice the torso.

If someone punches you in the face and breaks your nose, you could easily separate yourself from the assailant. But claiming someone else caused your pain does not change the simple fact that *it's your pain*. It reveals your condition and says little or nothing about whoever caused it.

An awareness of non-duality eliminates divisive subject-object dichotomies — me-or-you, us-or-them, winners-or-losers — that fuel conflict and hostility. Accepting a non-dual view of reality can encourage us to feel safer by replacing loneliness, alienation and competition with harmonious cooperation.

A Special Ignorance

We can easily become so distracted by our *monkey minds,* we become unaware of the world, our feelings and our thoughts. At times, we've all found ourselves continuing to idle at a traffic light after it's turned green.

It's frustrating to forget where we left our keys or parked the car at the shopping mall, or wonder whether we locked the door or turned off the stove before leaving the house. Yet a poor memory is not the issue. Because awareness is essential to intelligence and the formation of each memory, unawareness is a special ignorance. When we behave without conscious awareness, there is no mental impress to recall.

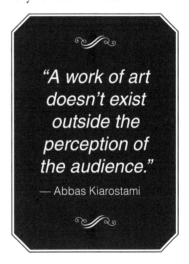

"A work of art doesn't exist outside the perception of the audience."

— Abbas Kiarostami

It's striking to watch people take one step off an escalator, then fail to move aside, completely unaware that others are riding behind them; or watching commuters push onto a crowded train or elevator before allowing departing riders to exit. Such people are not obtuse. They are oblivious.

Much of our unawareness is taken for granted. When you look at rows of telephone poles, do you see tall trees stripped of their branches and foliage? Ever wonder where plastic comes from? Have you considered why dead cow meat is called beef and pig flesh is pork? How is pre-heating an oven different than heating an oven? Why do the words *inflammable* and *flammable* mean the same thing? And though we know the Earth is spinning, why do we continue to speak about the sun, moon and stars rising in the East and setting in the West?

Awareness is not an all-or-nothing proposition. It is variable — a matter of degree. People with low self-awareness are often viewed as poorly educated, unreasonable or foolish. But more often than not, they are simply living, half-asleep in the gloomy shadows of unawareness.

A YouTube video by Monty Python's John Cleese went viral in 2014 with a derisive but humorous version of this imbroglio. Commenting on the Hollywood film and TV industry, Cleese explains, *"The problem with people like this is that they are so stupid, they have no idea how stupid they are. You see, if you're absolutely no good at something at all, then you lack exactly the skills you need to know that you're absolutely no good at it."*

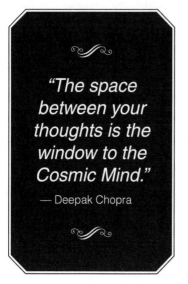

"The space between your thoughts is the window to the Cosmic Mind."

— Deepak Chopra

Two social psychologists from Cornell University, Dr. David Dunning and Dr. Justin Kruger, published research in 1999 about the tendency of people to overestimate their own competence. The basic tenet of the Dunning-Kruger Effect is, *"The less you know, the more you think you know, and the less you believe there is to know."* It's also called *"The American Idol Effect"* after the countless inept singers who are convinced they are the next Beyoncé or Michael Jackson. A few years after his study was released, Dunning summed it up with, *"One should pause to worry about one's own certainty, not the certainty of others."*

Life Is But a Dream

Self-evaluation is biased by a lack of awareness, beginning with a childish need to please others. One night many years ago, a dream revealed how simple-minded I'd been about this.

As a large crowd milled about, a disembodied voice told me these people were exclusively responsible for my dream — that I had nothing to do with it. I was shocked to learn my life was only an effect of what others thought. However, with reflection upon awakening, I realized I had been depending on other people to provide my self-worth, self-respect and self-confidence.

The poet Arthur Rimbaud cautioned us not to perceive ourselves through the eyes of others, writing, *"I is someone else."* Because the words *awareness* and *consciousness* are so similar in meaning, it's ironic that *self-aware* refers to the security found in accepting our individuality, while *self-conscious* implies a fear of what others might think of us.

My dream offered me a clear choice. So I appointed myself the president of my fan club, captain of my ship and master of my destiny. Initially, I was concerned about becoming over-confident, even pompous or arrogant. Yet I soon discovered that the more responsible I was for my life and affairs, the better I understood myself and the more I liked the parts of me hidden by my confusion and fear. In time, my new self-awareness made me more humble, enhanced my values and developed my interest in empathy, compassion and ancient wisdom teachings.

So, what can we do to become more self-aware? What is the secret to authentic self-observation and the discovery of our uniqueness? What should we examine — thoughts, emotional feelings, physical feelings, attitudes, beliefs, behavior, our impact on others?

Thinking is overvalued. Excessive thinking often causes more problems than it solves. A poem titled the *Centipede's Dilemma* (Katherine Craster, 1841–1874) illustrates the point.

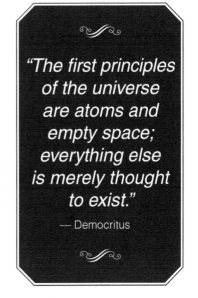

"The first principles of the universe are atoms and empty space; everything else is merely thought to exist."

— Democritus

"A centipede was happy — quite!
Until a toad in fun
Said, '*Pray, which leg moves after which?*'
This raised her doubts to such a pitch,
She fell exhausted in the ditch
Not knowing how to run. "

For centuries, sages, shamans and gurus have insisted that limiting our search for merit or substance to logical reasoning leads to self-deception. Instead, both objective and subjective realities are most clearly perceived in the intuitive feelings and insight that persist in the still, quiet gaps between our thoughts. Logic is best used, then, to validate our intuition.

Intentional Versus Unintentional Thought

It's one thing to deliberately think through a particular task, but task-unrelated thought (TUT) or *monkey mind* generates confusion and little else. To avoid becoming ensnared in random and chaotic thought, we must learn to step back and watch our unintentional thoughts unfold without judging or analyzing them.

Intrusive, unintentional thinking is an intrinsic and unavoidable phenomenon of mind. The unconscious mind generates streams of thoughts, some of which bubble up into awareness as pictures, words or sensations. And yet awareness endures with or without thought or feeling. Even the strange sensation of *drawing a blank* for a moment or two doesn't cause us to lose consciousness. Instead, we experience some degree of awareness of the expanding spaces between our thoughts.

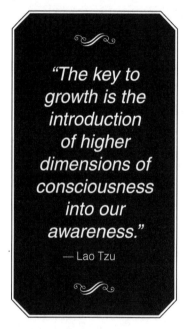

"The key to growth is the introduction of higher dimensions of consciousness into our awareness."

— Lao Tzu

Thoughts are unnecessary to living. The essence of what it means to be alive is awareness — to be conscious, alert, interested, sensitive and responsive.

Life is aware of itself and curious about its environment, even at a cellular level. Many single-celled organisms swim, find food, learn, remember and procreate without a brain, nervous system or even a single neuron. Although the origins of conscious awareness remain a mystery, we know our physical bodies are made of the same material elements as the planets and stars. Astronomer Carl Sagan has written, *"All of the rocky and metallic material we stand on, the iron in our blood, the calcium in our teeth, the carbon in our genes were produced billions of years ago in the interior of a red giant star. We are made of star-stuff."*[41]

Humans are remarkably complex life forms with awareness, perception, tactile and emotional feelings, conscience, intuition, imagination, logic and volition. So reality is more than physical energy and matter. There is Life — conscious and aware of its existence.

116

Awareness is the *Kingdom Within* — the Spirit or energy that animates and illumines us. All life is aware, but only to relative degrees. A commitment to personal development can expand awareness and raise our consciousness.

Eureka Illumination and Stress Reduction

Humans have always wondered about sudden illumination — the *aha breakthrough*, epiphany, revelation, inspiration or *second thought,* which bursts into awareness, spontaneously and full-blown. The experience is common, yet few people consider the significance of ideation, insight and intuition arriving with such clarity and self-assurance.

The wisdom expressed through intuition appears to arrive *from* the unconscious mind, but many sensitive, self-aware people suggest their intuition comes *through* the unconscious mind from their elevated spiritual self. Psychologists label this immortal essence the *transpersonal self,* while philosophers, theologians and mystics are more likely to use terms like *overshadowing soul, higher self* or *spirit.* It is important to recognize that any effort to access intuition with logical, rational thought impedes intuitive insight and understanding.

Consider the memory phenomenon known as the *tip of the tongue* or *presque vu.* The harder we try to recall some word, phrase or idea — even when it feels almost comprehensible — the more it eludes our awareness. And yet mere seconds after releasing the effort and moving on with our trains of thought — *Aha!* — awareness bursts open, revealing the information we were trying to recall.

The adage that *"the harder we try, the worse we do"* is a long-established cornerstone of sports psychology, sometimes called *"paralysis by analysis."* Expanded awareness, like physical performance, is a relaxation skill. Comprehension and understanding are greatly enhanced when the physical body feels safe and relaxed, the emotions are calm and the mind is quiet and still.

The Innate Wisdom Masked by Fear and Heartache

Fear is a doorway to understanding yourself better. The secret is in learning to plumb the depth and breadth of your anxiety in relaxed levels of expanded awareness. Becoming more self-aware reveals the personal wisdom hidden within heartache and upset.

As we understand our self better, we become less alienated and more content — calmer, happier and more self-confident. Fewer random thoughts distract us. This or that occurs as this *and* that. Behavior becomes less reflexive — more appropriate, even-tempered and well reasoned. Soon, defensiveness yields to acceptance and competition surrenders to cooperation — lines fade, borders dissolve and our perspective expands to include the *Wholeness* of Life.

I was in my mid-to-late 30s when the ragged pieces of my life finally fell into place. I was sitting quietly with my eyes closed, relaxing to better sort though some vague thoughts that had been troubling me. I had no particular agenda, and I'm not sure the word *meditation* would even apply. Suddenly, an inner voice interrupted my train of thought. As clearly as if seated beside me, a man's voice — in a half-whisper that carried a kind but authoritative tone — told me, *"The best parts of you are hidden where you're most afraid to look."*

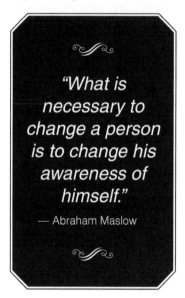

"What is necessary to change a person is to change his awareness of himself."

— Abraham Maslow

A resolute silence followed as if time had frozen over. I repeated the sentence to myself to ensure I'd remember it. But I quickly realized my revelation was too profound to ever forget. I was transformed. I felt awakened. And as successive weeks became months, I understood my life would never be the same.

I was no longer frightened by fear. For the first time in my life, I knew where to find the answers to my problems — inside my deepest fears.

My fear and heartache became a map and compass for discovering my best qualities, talents and abilities. I had found strength in my vulnerability. My full capacity to love and be loved was patiently waiting for me to find my way through the miasma of confusion and ignorance.

It was now clear that the only way out of pain — whether emotional or physical — is directly through it. There was no end run around it, no way over or under it. I had learned to face my fear and heartache, feel it fully, understand it and then release it.

I stopped comparing myself to others and turned within. Robert Frost's *"road less traveled"* now meant much more to me. Rather than avoid my fear, I recognized it as a road sign pointing out *The Way* to love, truth, wisdom and understanding. The unfolding of our true nature begins the moment we confront fear and ignorance. I would need to follow my heartache to find my heart.

Self-awareness Inventory

Developing self-awareness can be as easy as interviewing yourself, provided you ask the right questions. It's a good idea to write your answers to the following questions so that you may re-read them from time to time and make additions as needed.

This list is not exhaustive, just a good place to begin. Find a quiet place. Turn off your phone, relax and trust your first impression as you ask yourself:

- What do I care about?
- Why do I care about these things?
- What do I want most of all?
- Why do I want it?
- What do I hate having to do?
- What makes me furious?
- What makes me tired?
- What makes me happy?
- What do I spend too much time worrying about?
- Why do I worry about that?
- What frightens me?
- What helps me feel safe and relaxed?
- What would make me feel ultimately successful?
- What do I wish other people understood about me?
- If an epitaph were written for my tombstone, what would I like it to say?

"With awareness come responsibility and choice."
— Amanda Lindhout

Although we can learn from asking ourselves any number of personal questions, the greatest insight comes from contemplating the questions we typically avoid.

The Seduction of Fear

Two striking absurdities need clarification. The first is the belief that fear helps us to be careful and safe. The second is the inverse assumption that feeling safe makes us vulnerable to danger. Both are false.

Feeling safe and relaxed boosts awareness and intelligence, which makes us more alert, smarter and safer. The silly belief that fear makes us safe comes from confusing physical tension with control. However, 50 years of research in sports psychology has proven that strength, power, coordination and endurance are relaxation skills.

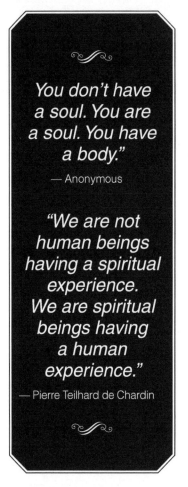

You don't have a soul. You are a soul. You have a body."

— Anonymous

"We are not human beings having a spiritual experience. We are spiritual beings having a human experience."

— Pierre Teilhard de Chardin

Feeling truly safe, happy and content can be frightening for those who are unfamiliar with the experience. Typically, they prefer the familiarity of the tension and discontent they know so well. You can release the false habit of conflating muscular tension with control by repeating the affirmation, *"I am in control of letting go of tension to feel safe and relaxed."*

"People have a hard time letting go of their suffering," writes the Vietnamese Zen teacher Thich Nhat Hanh. *"Out of a fear of the unknown, they prefer suffering that is familiar."* Psychotherapist and author Sheldon B. Kopp describes the lure of fear and heartache as: *"preferring the security of known misery to the misery of unfamiliar insecurity."*

Similarly, the Narcotics Anonymous book states, *"Many of us cling to our fears, doubts, self-loathing or hatred because there is a certain distorted security in familiar pain. It seems safer to embrace what we know than to let go of it for fear of the unknown."*

Further, fear can seem exciting and vital. There is little difference in the way *"Oh, no,"* and *"Oh, boy,"* feel in the body. Symptoms common to both include weak knees, girded loins, nervous stomach, heart palpitations, lump in the throat and sweaty palms. A few slow, deep breathes with an overall feeling of letting go of muscular tension converts anxiety into enthusiasm and a sense of adventure.

Relative and Absolute Truth

The more frightened, confused and unaware we become, the more likely we are to see the world in absolute, binary terms. Psychologists use the term *"splitting"* to refer to the fight-or-flight reflex inhibiting cognitive efforts to view dissimilar values as non-threatening and inclusive.

Routine anxiety, stress and fear also fosters childish defense mechanisms that suppress hurtful emotions — tactics like denial, the aloofness known as *"the cold shoulder"* or the smug, *"I don't care"* attitude. Tragically, attempts to quash any feeling cause the suppression of all feelings — happiness and joy, as well as heartache and sadness.

Clinging to fear as if it protects us or helps us to be careful also promotes the debilitating *us versus them mentality* — all or nothing, this or that, good or bad, right or wrong — with nothing in between. It rarely occurs to people to face fear and look for the relative truth in it. Most never get past the binary *"good guy, bad guy"* split, and fail to consider the overriding truth that everyone has light, shadow and many shades of gray within them.

> *You are, in fact, part of the glorious oneness of the universe. Everything beautiful in the world is within you."*
> — Russell Brand

Frightened people defend their viewpoints as if all differences are opposites. They feel opposed and threatened by any disagreement to any degree, and refuse to acknowledge the concept of *"agree to disagree."* They are likely to view their beliefs as thoroughly correct and good, while every variation, combination or permutation must be completely wrong and bad.

Imagine one fine day in January, my Hawaiian friend, Pekelo, meets my Alaskan friend, Joe, at my home in Los Angeles. The temperature is 62° F (≈17° C). Pekelo says he's chilly and asks to borrow a jacket. Joe is wearing a T-shirt and insists the weather is balmy. Who's right?

Perhaps you eat beef, but not dog meat. Other people eat dogs, but respect the cow as sacred. Who's right? The vegan says they're both wrong. Many gardeners think nothing of poisoning rodents and snails in their vegetable patch, but become upset when their family dog dies from ingesting the same toxic pellets.

Absolute truth is elusive. Proofs, facts and truths do exist in math and science, at least until contradicted by new information. For example, quantum physicists are now challenging even the fundamental assumption that the speed of light is a constant 186,000 miles per second.

Is it not possible for scientists and mathematicians to search for absolute truths, while personal values, ethics, morality and perspectives are seen as relatively true? While the final score of a football game may be absolutely undisputable, questions of how well each team played can remain matters of relative opinion.

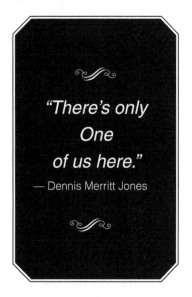

"There's only
One
of us here."

— Dennis Merritt Jones

People with low self-awareness may cry out for the clear certainty of absolutism, but it does not exist. In philosophy, the only Absolute is the One Life — the harmony and unity of All Things in the Cosmos.

Love as Awareness

Human fear and ignorance are at the core of all problems, so expanded awareness and understanding stand at the heart of all solutions. Wisdom respects the relative merit of all ideas. Aristotle touched on this when he wrote, *"It is the mark of an educated mind to be able to entertain a thought without accepting it."*

To recognize love as awareness and fear as unawareness sheds light upon Christ's admonitions to, *"Love your enemy ... turn the other cheek ... resist not evil."* In other words, the physical relaxation engendered by faith and fearlessness fosters awareness, insight and understanding. Those who limit the meaning of love to an emotional affinity will always struggle with this basic concept of Christianity.

"Love your enemy" refers to awareness redeeming fear, confusion and ignorance. Most religious scholars recognize Spiritual Love as awareness, insight, healing, faith, fearlessness and wisdom — qualities that are much more refined than emotional love, which generates a full range of feeling

from ecstatic bliss to devastating heartache, abandonment and grief.

When taken too literally, the Biblical phrase *"God fearing"* is also misunderstood. The Hebrew word for fear *(yirah)* means *reverence* and *awe*. Notice the conflicting meanings in the words *awesome* and *awful*. Consider, too, the scriptures: *"For God hath not given us the spirit of fear; but of power and of love and of a sound mind"* (2 Timothy 1:7); also, *"There is no fear in love; but perfect love casts out fear"* (1 John 4:18); and yet *"The fear of Jehovah is the beginning of wisdom"* (Psalm 111:10). So while emotional love may break your heart, love as awareness is healing wisdom — redeeming all heartache, ignorance and fear. And that is **Fearless Intelligence**.

It is impossible to hate hatred, though we may find it disgraceful, even contemptible. In writing, *"Darkness cannot drive out darkness: only light can do that. Hate cannot drive out hate: only love can do that,"* Dr. Martin Luther King Jr. was not speaking of love as an emotion, but as awareness and compassion. Anger and hatred are not substantial and cannot exist when exposed to the light of love as awareness, healing and understanding.

Exercises:

Commit to monitoring your self-talk. Listen carefully to your internal self-criticism. What part of you surfaces to contradict negative thinking? If these two arguments are you, then who is listening? Who decides which internal voice to accept and which to reject?

Practice sorting and naming your emotional feelings as you become aware of them. For example, notice how much easier it is to manage anger when you admit, *"I'm angry"* or *"I'm becoming angry."* Then, go deeper. Ask yourself, *"Is my anger made up of frustration? Does the frustration hurt? Does it feel desperate or sad? Am I using anger as a defensive shield?"* And ultimately, *"What fear is at the root of these feelings?"*

123

CHAPTER 7 —
THE TOOLS AND
TECHNIQUES OF INTUITIVE
INTELLIGENCE

Surmounting the basic trials of survival, civilization and technology,
a new domain is emerging — the Kingdom of Conscious Souls.
To prepare, we must replace impulse and instinct
with the refined insight of mindful intuition.

I've enjoyed backyard barbecuing all my life. Open-flame cooking sears a delectable, smoky flavor into food that can't be matched. It's like camping, but with the added convenience of an adjoining kitchen with a refrigerator, sink and running water.

The downside is the charcoal. I never liked having to deal with the bulky bags and filthy carbon dust. The briquettes are difficult to light, plus there's a 20-minute wait until ash covers the coals.

So I was excited when I bought my first propane barbecue. No more dirty charcoal, just convenient, clean-burning gas on demand. I became proficient at blending a variety of custom marinades — a few tablespoons of cooking oil, a splash of something acidic, like wine, vinegar or citrus juice and a sprinkling of my favorite herbs and spices. Shake vigorously and *voilà* — a custom marinade and basting sauce.

One day about five years after purchasing my propane grill, I opened the gas valve, lit the flame and closed the lid to raise the heat before cooking. As I walked back into my house, an ominous, shadowy feeling of fear and danger swept over me. Though sudden and brief, it was a dreadfully strong sensation.

I was mystified and anxious, yet curious. Since I had a few minutes while the barbeque was heating, I sat down on my sofa to reflect on what had just happened.

I had no recollection of ever having experienced anything like it and found no logical reason for feeling so threatened. I closed my eyes, took a deep breath and relaxed as I exhaled.

A decade earlier, I had learned about the alpha brainwave level while attending a 40-hour Silva Mind Control course. Alpha is a mindful, receptive brainwave state between deep sleep and wide awake — a relaxed zone in which emotions soften, mental alertness is enhanced and self-awareness naturally expands.[42]

As often happens in alpha, colorful imagery soon floated against the black background of my closed eyelids. Yielding to the daydream, I relaxed further and directed my attention to the bottomless dismay I had felt moments before.

Suddenly, an instantaneous knowing exploded into my awareness. It began with echoes of my mother scolding me: *"If you take care of it, it will last forever."*

My heart sank as a deep, stabbing grief eviscerated me. My mind was flooded by, *"This is how it feels to know you're dying"* — though I knew I was in no danger.

Moments later, I realized it was my barbeque that was dying. Over the years, I had failed to notice the gradual accumulation of grease, grime and rust. That momentary flash of fear was telling me my treasured barbeque would soon be junk. But there was more.

My awareness spilled over with profound insight and understanding about the impermanence of material things — even the transience of thought and feeling. As a child, I had taken my mother's admonition too literally. Physical objects do *not* endure. And like material forms, thoughts and feelings are transient. So the satisfaction of possessing desirable things also fades.

Only energy is eternal. The voice of my high school physics teacher, Mr. Britain, reverberated in my brain: *"Matter is energy condensed into decaying, impermanent forms. Energy, however, can neither be created nor destroyed."*

Logic and Intuition

That brief dagger of fear became a life-changing gift. Not only did I better understand the impermanence of things, I also realized the value of intuition for interpreting emotional feelings.

Fear and anger challenge us to justify our right to be hurt and upset. Yet attempts to understand hurtful emotions with logic inhibit insight while sustaining discomfort. The language of feelings is intuition.

I had tried to understand my emotions logically until I realized rumination is actually a resistance to feeling. My emotional feelings were not cryptic or confusing, but what I *thought* about them was incomprehensible.

There is no one to blame for hurtful feelings. We are each responsible for our suffering, but not at fault. We must *feel* our heartache and acknowledge its presence without judgment or self-blame. Then, in relaxed, intuitive states, become open and receptive to everything it reveals about us.

> *"You must train your intuition — you must trust the small voice inside you which tells you exactly what to say, what to decide."*
>
> — Ingrid Bergman

Intuition is the highest intelligence — the most extraordinary and exquisite benefit of becoming more self-aware. It is the wisdom of the heart, divulging insight, understanding and astonishing, unimaginable levels of comprehension. Yet the still, small voice of intuition is almost impossible to hear above the din of our frenzied, frightened and stressed ego — a disorder we must learn to manage.

What Is Stress?

Stress results from routine adversity as well as acute and chronic over-stimulation. The concept was coined in 1936 by Dr. Hans Selye, who defined it as *"the non-specific response of the body to any demand for change."*

Though still considered to be primarily a physical response, in a more comprehensive way, stress is a full cycle of mental confusion and emotional heartache that suppresses the immune system and causes more stress. Supported by low self-esteem and poor self-image, stress degrades self-awareness causing even greater confusion and emotional hurt.

The consequences of unmanaged anxiety and stress range from mild apprehension to clinical disorders that include panic attacks, phobias, obsessive-compulsive disorder (OCD), post-traumatic stress disorder (PTSD), attention deficit hyperactivity disorder (ADHD), as well as depression, anger, low self-confidence, poor self-esteem and a distrust of self and others.

Technically, anxiety is termed fear only when obvious danger is imminent. However, the unconscious (subconscious) mind does not distinguish between real or imagined circumstances. So there's no significant distinction between anxiety and fear. Stress refers to the dynamic cycle of fear or anxiety creating confusion, which leads to more fear and more confusion.

Out of this fear, anxiety and stress, a variety of hurtful emotions rise up as useful symptoms. Remember, as stated earlier, upsetting and frustrating feelings are called *negative emotions* only because they hurt. In fact, they are replete with helpful information, just like physical pain.

What Are Emotions?

Emotional feelings overlap our mental and physical faculties. They are felt in the physical body as interactions — both causes and effects — of our mental thoughts. Emotions are complex and inter-reliant. For example, anger contains hurt, sadness, frustration and fear. Love includes happiness, kindness, peace, ethics and aesthetic appreciation.

Bubbling up from the unconscious self, networks of emotions interact with our thoughts to create whole tapestries of moods and attitudes. Similar life experiences are seen in very different ways as each individual's disposition filters, distorts and shapes daily events into personal dramas and traumas.

All feelings, physical and emotional, are personal responses. Others can cause us to hurt, but it's always our pain. Hurt, soreness and discomfort tell us about our own condition, not the person who stimulated our pain. Even empathy relies on our understanding of how we feel or have felt.

We can avoid being victims of our emotions by exploring the roots of our anxiety. As we unearth their buried meanings, we can recognize, understand and manage hurtful emotions and choose appropriate and creative responses.

Emotions motivate behavior *(from Latin = emotus, to move out, stir up, agitate)*, whether intentional or as reflexive reactions with little thought at all. Positive feelings drive thoughts into action. Negative emotions caution against adverse results, but also contain positive clues for resolution when discerned intuitively.

The most effective means of understanding emotional feelings is much different than our typical consideration of ideas and beliefs. Emotions do not submit to logical analysis. They require intuitive intelligence. Efforts to process emotions rationally are not only futile, they are counter-productive. Logic and judgment suppress emotional awareness.

Emotions are called feelings because they are felt in the physical body, much like physical pleasure and discomfort. This helps explain why bottled-up emotions often express themselves as physical aches and pains, particularly in the back, shoulders and neck.[43]

Our ideas and beliefs call for logic and reasoning, but our emotions must be felt and discerned intuitively. The techniques that follow will help you develop your intuition to reveal the meaning of your emotional feelings.

A circle of basic emotions was developed in the 1980s by psychologist Dr. Robert Plutchik that contrasts four pairs of basic feelings — happiness vs. sadness, anger vs. fear, trust vs. disgust, and surprise vs. anticipation. Studies of facial expressions have led many psychologists to drop trust and anticipation in favor of a six-emotion model. Besides happiness and positive surprise, the others are all distressing — fear, anger, sadness and disgust.

Research by the Institute of Neuroscience and Psychology at the University of Glasgow suggests that, whether welcomed or upsetting, surprise is a fear response, and disgust is a form of anger. If so, there are only four basic emotions — happiness, fear, anger and sadness. However, many psychologists and sociologists view human emotions as far too complex for such simple models.

It is important to point out that love is not included in these lists of emotional feelings. Love is generally regarded to be a primal drive that engenders a full range of emotions, from ecstasy to agony.

Intuition and Emotional Self-awareness

Self-awareness begins with acceptance, meaning, *"to acknowledge reality."* Acceptance is not surrender or appeasement. It is a sensible starting point for conscious responses. There is no benefit in wishing things were not as they are or ruminating over unanswerable *"Why me?"* questions.

Nothing is gained from wallowing in the despair of feeling sorry for yourself or becoming angry at life's unfairness. Instead of judging and analyzing your emotions with logical thought, relax and feel them fully, especially when they hurt or upset you.

Though you may not be aware of it, you can suspend thinking to enhance the feeling of emotions in your body. For example, we can hear music while we think. In fact, students often use music to reduce distraction while studying. But to truly *listen* to music — to become swept away or lost in the music — we must intentionally suspend our logic.

People who love music often do this unconsciously. But listening to music to experience thought-free feelings is a marvelous practice for expanding awareness. In just a few more pages, we'll explain this technique in detail.

Intuition Is Not Instinct

The common assumption that instinct and intuition are identical must be reconsidered. Like two sides of the same coin, instinct and intuition are compatible in their unconscious spontaneity but divergent as methods of understanding.

Both are visceral but emanate from different nerve centers. Instinct is centered in the solar plexus (gut feeling). It is a fear-based, problem-oriented sense that we share with the animal kingdom (herd or mob mentality, killer instinct) that signals unawareness, confusion and potential danger.

Intuition is heart-centered — a love-based, solution-oriented realization that appears to be uniquely human. Instinct warns us with *"Oh, no. Run away,"* feelings, while intuition enlightens us with *"Oh, boy. Move toward,"* feelings and comprehensive insight.

The edifying nature of intuition is not illogical, but it is non-logical. Instead of resulting from analytical reasoning, intuitive intelligence arrives as holistic illumination. Sometimes the revelation arrives slowly, as in *"the dawning of a new idea."* Other times the illumination snaps into our brains like a light bulb being switched on. Occasionally, we are thunderstruck by an explosive epiphany.

In the Third Century BCE, the Greek philosopher Archimedes exclaimed, *"Eureka! Eureka!" (I have found it!)* as he luxuriated in a warm bath. In a flash of insight, he realized the volume of an irregularly shaped object could be determined by measuring the amount of water displaced when it was submerged.

Many other famous examples of *"aha illumination"* also involve relaxed alpha brainwave states. Albert Einstein uncovered hidden secrets of the universe in his mind's eye with purposeful daydreams.

> *"The intuitive mind is a sacred gift and the rational mind is a faithful servant. We have created a society that honors the servant and has forgotten the gift."*
>
> — Bob Samples

Much has been written about Thomas Edison catnapping at his desk, though in fact, he was visualizing his inventions with hypnagogic imagery. Placing metal plates on the floor beneath each hand, Edison held large ball bearings as he daydreamed. Anytime he fell asleep, the clang of the steel balls hitting the plates would wake him, so he could resume his conscious visualizations.

Many of Edgar Allan Poe's tales of horror came to him as nightmares, and Mary Shelley admitted her ideas for Frankenstein *"haunted her midnight pillow"* for months. Countless songwriters have confessed to dreaming up melodies while asleep. Paul McCartney's *Yesterday* and *Let It Be* were received in dreams, as was John Lennon's *#9 Dream*, Jimi Hendrix's *Purple Haze*,

Keith Richard's *Satisfaction,* Sting's *Every Breath You Take* and R.E.M.'s *It's the End of the World as We Know It.*

Dmitri Mendeleev conceived the periodic table for organizing chemical elements in a dream. August Kekulé's vision of the six-sided benzene ring and Elias Howe's idea of threading a sewing machine needle at the pointed end occurred in dreams. Nobel laureate James Watson admits his dream about a spiral staircase led to his discovery of the double-helix structure of DNA molecules.

Everyone becomes much more receptive to intuitive intelligence when relaxed, whether during night dreams, daydreams, guided imagery, meditation, prayer, contemplation or a mindfulness practice. Consider, too, how unlikely we are to enjoy meaningful insight or understanding during stressful situations, such as the mind-numbing performance anxiety of public speaking or sitting for an academic exam.

Intuitive insight requires safe, relaxed states of mind. We're not likely to have an intense argument with a friend or family member interrupted by a burst of creative insight. Emotional confusion is a vicious cycle spiraling downward into less and less awareness.

Intuitive intelligence differs from logic in four ways.

Intuition — Originates in the Unconscious Mind	*Logic — A Product of the Conscious Mind*
Intuition is holistic and complete. (Emotional EQ)	Logic reduces general concepts to specific parts. (Mental IQ)
Intuition arrives full-blown as if an unconscious conclusion has suddenly been revealed.	Logic moves in degrees, one linear step at a time.
The slightest stress or apprehension destroys receptivity to intuition.	The logical mind is much more resilient to the debilitating effects of stress.
Intuitive insight is veridical and accompanied by a sense of confirmation.	Logical assumptions are often incorrect or incomplete.

By using our intuition to understand hurtful emotions, the meaning and purpose of heartache can be revealed and the discomfort released. If irritation or frustration persists, just acknowledge the insight gained to that point, then repeat the intuitive intelligence techniques from the pages that follow.

Mindfulness Meditation

Learning to live in the present moment with non-judgmental acceptance requires a proper meditation practice. Known throughout Asia as vipassana or insight meditation, the objective of mindfulness meditation is expanded self-awareness, also termed as higher consciousness.

Mindfulness provides countless benefits. Stress-based frenzy, known to meditators as monkey mind, is commonly misdiagnosed as attention deficit hyperactivity disorder (ADHD). Mindful self-awareness extends attention span and diminishes racing thoughts.

Mindfulness improves empathy and interpersonal communication. It promotes pain control, accelerates healing and normalizes blood pressure by reducing the stress hormones adrenaline and cortisol. Mindfulness is an effective treatment for anger management, depression and post-traumatic stress disorder (PTSD). A mindfulness practice helps us substitute equanimity for reflexive reactions. And perhaps most importantly, it greatly improves intuition, allowing us to manage our emotional feelings for expanded insight and understanding.

The initial step of any meditation training involves learning to feel physically relaxed and safe. In the second exercise, you will practice watching your body breathe itself. Next, you'll put your attention on your thought streams — the incessant inner narratives, sometimes called self-talk or the internal monologue. These are the spontaneous thoughts that petition your attention after you have ceased deliberate thinking. And in the fourth step, you will shift your attention to emotional hurt to elevate and expand self-awareness.

Exercise #1 — Progressive Muscular Relaxation

This is a simple but effective technique. Read and study the following paragraphs, then close your eyes and practice the exercise to the best of your recollection. As you become more experienced and proficient, you'll need to review these instructions less often. If you wish, you can slowly speak this narrative into an audio recorder, computer or phone app for playback during your meditation. The easiest option would be to listen to the audiobook version of **Fearless Intelligence**.

You may sit cross-legged on the floor, a meditation pillow or a bench, although most people are more comfortable on a chair or sofa. Sit straight, but not rigid. Balance your head and shoulders above your spine and hips. Relax and let go of muscular tension. Spend a few moments feeling the furniture support your body. Then move your attention to feeling the floor beneath your feet.

Close your eyes and imagine how a tree or flower feels to be deeply rooted in the ground. Sense how you might feel if you also had roots extending from your ankles and feet, through your shoes and the floor, deep into the warm, fertile soil. Feel grounded and plugged into the earth, as if you belong here. This is where you grow. You are in your place.

Slightly tense the muscles in your feet for just a couple of seconds, and then let go. In the same way, gently tighten your calf muscles for just a few seconds, and then feel a similar release.

Having reminded yourself how letting go feels, shift your awareness back to your feet. Although they are already relaxed, see if you can sense just a little more relaxation in your feet. Then, although your calves are also relaxed, see if you can also feel a further letting go below your knees — muscles unwinding, becoming loose and limp. Imagine feeling nervous energy, stress and anxiety draining from your legs down into the earth.

Lift your attention to your upper legs and inhale slowly and deeply through your nose. Hold for just a moment as your breath peaks. Then as you slowly exhale through your nose, feel the quadriceps muscles at the top of your upper legs relax. After inhaling another slow, deep breath, feel the hamstring muscles along the back of your thighs letting go as you exhale.

Continue to take slow, deep breaths through your nose. Each time you exhale, imagine sending that breath into the next area you wish to relax — your buttocks, your lower back and abdomen, your mid-back and stomach as you move up through the center of your torso. Feel your body becoming more and more relaxed.

Remind yourself that you are in control of this letting go, especially if you have confused muscular tension with control before now. Physical tension is not armor and does not protect or enhance control. Tight muscles make us weaker. Overall power, coordination and control come from relaxation and slow, mindful breathing. Remember, *"Tension reduces awareness. Relaxation expands awareness."*

Lift your attention into your rib cage. Imagine your lungs relaxing and allow your breathing to find its own rhythm. Tell yourself that all the organs in your upper body — heart, lungs, stomach, kidneys, liver, pancreas, gallbladder and spleen — are doing a better job with less effort as you become more and more relaxed.

Like butter on a warm day, feel yourself letting go. Luxuriate in the wonderful feelings of relaxation spreading across your shoulders and down into your arms. Continue through your elbows, forearms and into the back of your hands, your palms and all the way down to the tips of your fingers and thumbs. In your mind's eye, visualize the veins, arteries and capillaries throughout your body dilating, as you feel safer and more relaxed. Envision your blood-flow moving more freely — with less resistance — as you feel the deep letting go throughout your body.

Bring your attention to your neck and shoulders and feel relaxation spreading into the back of your head. You'll feel the space around your ears sag or droop slightly as you relax your scalp. Feel letting go in your forehead, behind your eyebrows, your eyelids and face. Finish by relaxing your jawbone (mandible) where it's hinged to your skull, just below your cheekbones.

Slowly and effortlessly, expand your conscious awareness to experience the full range of tranquility and ease throughout your body — from the top of your head to the soles of your feet. Allow a slight smile to gently lift the corners of your mouth. Pretend you can feel the warmth of the sun tenderly embracing your face and arms. Perhaps you could also feel a slight breeze, just a little cooler as if you were sitting in a paradise, a beautiful garden of perfect peace and ideal relaxation.

When you're ready to return to the waking state, simply form the intention in your mind, inhale slowly through your nose, and as you exhale, open your eyes, wide awake, alert, feeling fine — better than before.

Exercise #2 — Watching Your Body Breathe Itself

As you become familiar with the feelings of deep relaxation, you can relinquish the first exercise — progressive muscular relaxation. Read the following instructions each time you practice this second exercise until you are familiar with the tradition.

Begin each meditative breath-watching session by devoting 10 to 30 seconds to recalling how wonderful it feels to be deeply and fully relaxed, safe and at peace. Form a subtle smile and feel an elegant warmth spread over your body as every bit of residual stress and nervous anxiety drains into the ground.

Close your eyes and move your awareness to the bottom of your nose. Imagine you exist as a tiny spark of awareness on the ridgeline of cartilage between your nostrils. Deliberately breathe in and out through your nose, slowly and deeply, three or four times, and feel the gentle rush of air inside your nostrils.

Release your deliberate breathing and allow your body to breathe itself. Permit your body to set its own pace and depth and simply observe the air spilling over the rim of your nostrils. Instead of thinking of yourself as the breather, become the witness of your body breathing itself. Without any judgment whatsoever, simply experience your body breathing, all by itself.

Your mind will soon become disinterested and unintentionally pull your awareness away from your breathing to some sort of random thought. It may be a memory, a current issue or future concern. Do not admonish yourself, but simply acknowledge that thinking is what the mind does even when it is not engaged. Let go of the interruption and bring your attention back to the bottom of your nose. Resume your perception of your body breathing itself — all by itself.

Your goal is not to maintain concentration, but to be aware of distraction as it happens. As if you are patiently training a puppy to sit and stay, gently return your attention to your breathing, reminding yourself to remain relaxed and content.

As you continue to meditate upon your body breathing itself, follow the full range of your breath, from beginning to end. Passively watch your body instinctively inhale, pause briefly, exhale, pause, then inhale again. If you wish, you can think of your breathing as similar to the sliding valve on a trombone. But do not ride back and forth on your breath. Instead, maintain a detached sense of observing your breathing from a fixed point at the bottom of your nose.

You might compare your inhalation to waves gently rolling into the shoreline along a pond, lake or ocean. As you exhale, the water drains down the beach and back into the water. But as soon as you realize your thought-train has begun to sneak off in other directions, silently tell yourself, *"Thinking. I am thinking."* Let it go and return to watching your breath from that fixed point on the cartilage between your nostrils.

Anytime you are distracted by an external noise, like a neighbor's dog barking, tell yourself, silently and internally, *"Every time the dog barks, the sound will fade as I become more relaxed and focused."* Feel yourself letting go of muscular tension and emotional resentment and return to simply watching your body breathe itself free from all evaluation and judgment.

Consider the ebb and flow of your breath as cyclic. When you pedal a bicycle, your feet go around and around as your legs go up and down. Feel the in and out of your breathing transition to a smooth, cyclic sensation. Practice for 10 to 20 minutes each day for two to three weeks before moving to Exercise #3.

Exercise #3 — Watching Trains of Thought

Everyone is routinely distracted by random thoughts, whether reading, speaking, watching videos or driving a car, but not everyone is aware of it. Right now, pause your reading of this book and notice how quickly your mind leaps to its own restless agenda.

The thought trains drifting through our minds are an unconscious byproduct of the primitive limbic brain. Because it's survival-based, these impulsive thoughts are inevitably full of anxiety, worry and self-criticism. We cannot suppress these impulsive thoughts, but we can rise above them with expanded self-awareness.

As we learn to calm the mind in meditation, we gain the ability to examine emotional feelings and thoughts without reacting to them. Thoughts can be gently held in abeyance. The resulting opportunity to carefully study and contemplate their meanings and motives enables us to substitute even-tempered, levelheaded responses for reflexive reactions.

Having practiced the breath-watching exercise one- to two-dozen times, you should now be familiar with the experience of being consciously aware from an elevated point of view. In this next exercise, we will continue to raise your self-awareness from *being aware* to *Being Awareness*.

As we shift the focus of meditation from observing our breath to observing our train of thoughts, we must confront the distinction between cogitation (purposeful thought) and the unbroken trains of thought that persevere despite our intentions.

Thinking is what the mind does. Awake or asleep, thinking never ceases. Though our minds routinely move through various levels and states of awareness, thinking is linear. The mind cannot consider more than one thought at a time, yet it must always be thinking.

We can slow down our thought-stream, but we cannot stop it. Deep relaxation is the means for slowing and quieting the trains of thought that compete for our attention. Though coupled like railroad cars, the gaps between our thoughts begin to open during this type of meditation. So our first goal in Exercise #3 is to notice the gradual lengthening of the gaps between our spontaneous thoughts.

Underwater swimmers can hold their breath for only a limited time before their body involuntarily forces them to resume breathing. In the same way, spontaneous trains of thought not only distract us during purposeful thinking but also demand attention when we ignore them.

Imagine being unable to turn off your car's engine after driving from place to place. So it is with the mind. Thoughts and feelings idle endlessly without regard to our need or awareness. Awake or asleep, the mind worries, wishes, wonders and wanders.

Because few schools teach children about awareness, most of us, even as adults, view our spontaneous trains of thought as no different than deliberate thinking. In this third meditation exercise, we use relaxation to slow our involuntary monkey mind, allowing the gaps between our thoughts to expand. As one entire second, then two or even three seconds pass without thinking, you'll understand that your awareness is distinct from your thought process.

This is the distinction between being aware and *Being Awareness*. You are not the thinker or the breather. You are the awareness that can impartially witness your thoughts, feelings, behavior and perception. Though often misused and misunderstood, the word *meta-awareness* primarily means Being Awareness — self-aware that you are Awareness Itself.

As a side note, some academics conflate detachment and dissociation and then use the word meta-awareness or metacognition to refer to both. Generally, meditators view detachment as the mindfully enhanced awareness of their perception while remaining objectively dispassionate. Dissociation is an involuntary state of being less aware, semi-aware or unaware, e.g. readers often dissociate and lose awareness and comprehension even though their eyes continue to scan lines of print. On the other hand, an example of detachment would be to marvel at our ability to find deep meaning in the symbolism of printed words and phrases while they're being read and comprehended.

This next exercise is similar to the last, except we focus our attention on our involuntary trains of thought from a detached and elevated position of mindfulness. Again, the goal is not to stop your thoughts or avoid distraction, but simply to be aware of them. As you observe your mind drifting, let it wander wherever it wants without judgment. Be curiously fascinated by the associations, intervals and leaps of logic your mind makes as it aimlessly meanders. Above all, identify as the witness of your thought-process rather than the thinker.

In the same way as in Exercise #2, close your eyes, take a few slow, deep breaths and relax. After observing your breath for two or three minutes, effortlessly shift your awareness to your trains of thought. Gently center yourself upon this awareness for 10 to 20 minutes at least once each day in safe and relaxed states.

Recognize your natural ability to maintain awareness even during the gaps between your thoughts. For variety, you may also dedicate meditation sessions to focusing your attention on your emotional feelings or physical sensations in place of your thought-trains.

Exercise #4 — Listen to Music

This is a great technique for music lovers and those who are naturally auditory in the way they organize mental information — that is, those who are more likely to hear their thoughts than see them as images.

Play a tune you like, close your eyes and relax. If there are discernable lyrics, ignore them in favor of listening only to the instruments. In your first pass, listen only to the instrument playing the main theme or melody. Replay the tune and during the second pass, listen only to the fills, background and rhythm instruments. On the third pass, focus your attention only on the bass line, then the percussion instruments, horn section, and so on.

Each time your mind drifts from your intention, do not admonish yourself, but simply bring your attention back to the portion of the music you were focused upon. In this way, you can quickly learn to detach your self-awareness from the spontaneous thoughts that constantly petition us for attention. In time, you will awaken to the extraordinary freedom of identifying yourself as the observer of input rather than the thinking analyzer.

Daily Mindfulness

In time, your ever-improving ability to recognize the difference between deliberate consideration and background monkey mind will allow you to observe daily routines from a detached and more comprehensive viewpoint.

For example, devote a trip to the grocery store or post office to observing yourself driving to the exclusion of all other thought. Feel the steering wheel in your hands and the seat supporting your body. Consider what is happening in the car's transmission as you shift the gears. Feel the drive wheels pushing the car forward as you gently press the accelerator pedal toward the floor.

The pleasant and pleasurable feelings that result can also be found in mindfully walking — aware of each step … leg swinging, heel touching, rolling toward your toes, pushing off as the other leg swings by. And if this sounds a bit mundane and pointless, eat just one meal mindfully — no conversation, thinking of nothing but chewing, swallowing and absorbing the nutrients that find their way into your bloodstream, flowing to each and every cell in your body.

The Pay-off

As you practice stress reduction and mindfulness meditation, you will notice an ever-expanding awareness of events and circumstances in your daily life. Slowly, an elevated perspective of life as a magnificent tapestry will replace your existence on a linear timeline. You'll begin to experience all things beautifully interwoven in space and time, and liberate yourself from the distortion and opacity of feeling like a victim or target of life.

In time, you will see distinctions as relative rather than absolute. You-or-me will be redeemed to you-*and*-me. Conflicts will elegantly resolve themselves. Harmony replaces chaos and frenzy; and stress, anxiety, depression and pain — both physical and emotional — will subside.

For ages, mystics, prophets and shamans have used many different words to describe this state of expanded awareness — peace, wisdom, truth, compassion, nirvana, enlightenment, Christ consciousness, ecstasy and bliss. Yet for those who wish to go further — to the deeper meanings of awareness as Love — we have one additional technique and some additional information about emotional distress.

CHAPTER 8 —
THE FEELINGS DIALOGUE

By learning to relax and focus on our emotional feelings, we can perceive the extraordinary wisdom of our conscience, the voice of the soul.

No myth is more destructive than the belief that we are separate and essentially dissimilar beings. Like the idiom about *"not seeing the forest for the trees,"* we fail to recognize humanity as a single family or the global ecology as a unitary life support system.

Love is the self-evident solution to alienation, hostility and fear. Yet loving one another is viewed as a lofty, challenging goal, despite having been taught to *"love thy neighbor as thyself,"* including *"love your enemies."*

Religious bigotry, race hate and misogyny are sustained by the most insignificant distinctions. And the limbic brain's fight-or-flight reflex promotes worldviews twisted into false dichotomies — us or them, either this or that, and all or nothing.

This appearance of separation also leads us to believe we are victims of circumstance. We presume we are effects of a life done to us, so we look for the cause of our problems in the external world.

The natural world has no problems, only steadfast principles. Gravity, electromagnetism and thermodynamics have integrity. Situations we perceive as problematic are born and sustained entirely by our confusion, ignorance and unawareness.

There is wisdom in recognizing heartache, dismay and despair as personal responses that vanish in the presence of self-awareness. It is not the comfort of peace and love that heals and transforms, but the insight and understanding it offers.

The modern Western medical establishment linked emotions to mental health, even though ancient philosophers associated passion and sentiment with the physical body, where emotional sensations are felt. However, emotions are a blend of mental causes and physical effects — interactions that rise from the center of the mind-body connection.

With sufficient awareness, emotional feelings offer profound wisdom — insight that transcends the understanding provided by logic alone. Although unmanaged emotions can trigger illogical thoughts and regrettable behavior, we can learn to use safe, relaxed and calm states to reveal astute qualities of emotionally based comprehension and higher consciousness.

> *"One of the painful things about our time is that those who feel certainty are stupid, and those with any imagination and understanding are filled with doubt and indecision."*
>
> — Bertrand Russell

As subjective expressions of our individuality, the primary value of emotional intelligence is to become better and better at understanding our individuality. Further, as we recognize what makes us tick, our empathy and ability to manage relationships also grows. In both cases, the key to emotional awareness is its place between mental thought and physical behavior.

Our triune nature works best when intentional behavior results from lucid thoughts motivated by well-managed emotions. Yet commonly, we react reflexively with little or no thought — *"because I felt like it."* Thinking comes last as attempts to rationalize our behavior.

There's no question that thoughts and emotional feelings influence each other. Both cognitive-behavioral and rational-emotive schools of psychotherapy are based on the premise that thoughts produce emotional feelings. Yet it's also easy to see how emotions influence thinking.

The force of emotions drives the energy of thoughts into action. Our best behavior requires well-reasoned thoughts motivated by even-tempered emotions. Feelings we fail to carefully consider trigger unconscious and often-regrettable reactions. So we must learn to manage our emotional feelings with intuitive insight.

The Sequence: Thought, Feeling and Action

A calm, levelheaded state of self-awareness marked by lucid thinking and stable emotions is necessary for composure and self-control. A simple way to remember that clear thoughts plus enthusiastic feelings create optimal behavior is the slogan introduced in Chapter 1: *"Check it out, feel it out, act it out."*

With poor self-awareness, thoughts and feelings are easily conflated and confused. For example, statements like, *"I feel like I can't do that"* or *"I feel like I don't deserve it,"* are not emotional feelings. They are mental conclusions — judgments born of self-loathing and low self-esteem. Similarly, *"feeling guilty"* is not an emotion, but rather an unconscious decision resulting from thinking about feelings like shame, remorse or humiliation.

Also, using the expressions *"feel like"* and *"because"* are unconscious means of pivoting from uncomfortable feelings to the relative safety of objective thought. Saying, *"I feel like a failure,"* doesn't make it an emotional feeling. It, too, is a mental judgment.

People can be quite obtuse about their emotions. One counseling session that stands out in my memory involved a married couple we'll identify as Jim and Ellen. Near the end of their first session, I asked Ellen to tell Jim how she felt about the relationship. Looking down, as if into her body, she slowly listed the emotions she'd been feeling. *"Well, I feel hurt and confused, lonely ... abandoned, actually; also sad, depressed and angry."*

Turning to Jim, I suggested he tell Ellen how he felt about their marriage. Without hesitation, he turned and looked directly at his wife. *"I feel you're a bitch,"* he blurted. Before he could continue, I interrupted, *"No, Jim. That's not a feeling."*

"But that's how I feel," he argued. So I explained, *"Jim, 'You're a bitch' is not an emotion. It's a thought — a judgment with a lot of anger behind it."*

Jim continued to find it difficult, if not impossible, to take responsibility for his emotional feelings without blaming his wife or other people for *"making him feel"* as he did. Rather than see themselves as the source of their own emotions, victims view themselves only as targets or effects of a life that's being done to them.

Physical and Emotional Feelings

Just as physical pain and discomfort are often misdiagnosed, emotions are also difficult to understand when we rely on logical reasoning. We wouldn't search for the meaning of a Chinese word in an English dictionary, so why do we expect our thoughts to reveal the complexities of emotional sense and sensation? Mental keys don't unlock emotional doors. You would never reconcile your checkbook based on how you feel about your financial situation. It's no less absurd to try deciphering the meaning of your emotions with logical reasoning and analysis.

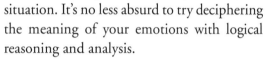

"Get out of your head and get into your heart. Think less, feel more."

— Osho

When I counsel and train private clients and students in emotional intelligence, I often ask them to close their eyes, take a few slow, deep breaths, relax and remember a time when they felt hurt, embarrassed, ashamed or humiliated. Once we've identified a strong memory, I tell them to, *"Make it seem real, as if it were happening right now. Take your time and tell me how you're feeling."*

I'm intrigued by how difficult this is for most people. They readily tell me what they think, but struggle to find words to describe how they feel, much less why.

Guiding my clients, I'll suggest, *"Move your awareness from your head down into your body. Tell me what you're feeling in your body."* They may begin with feeling words but soon pivot to thoughts.

"I feel empty. It's a dark, heavy, depressing feeling … and I'm angry, because … ." As mentioned, the word *"because"* takes us back to a mental analysis of our emotional feelings — a devious though largely unconscious means of avoiding the intuitive awareness feelings offer.

Again, let's be clear about the distinctions between mental thoughts and emotional feelings. Thoughts are reasonable, objective, fact-based inquiries and deliberations about the world. Emotions are personal, subjective and motivational responses — reflections of our individuality.

Both thoughts and emotional feelings bubble up into awareness from the unconscious mind. But unlike thoughts, emotions resist logical management. Attempts to understand your emotional heartache with rational thinking is just as flawed as the *"truthiness"* of using emotional feelings to understand the external world.[44] The belief that something is right because it *feels* right only applies to understanding yourself. Even empathetic attempts to understand how others feel are limited by how well we understand our own emotions.

Intuition, not logic, is the language of emotions and, therefore, the portal to wisdom. To become aware of anger, depression, envy or any other heartache while it's still a mile away — small and barely perceptible — we must first look into our physical body for the slightest somatic sensations triggered by emotions.

Our emotional hurt becomes calmer and easier to manage in quiet states of deep relaxation. So by consciously negating the tension of heartache and confusion with safe and calm responses, our emotions open to intuitive insight and understanding and become more amenable to transformation through suggestion.

Imagine a toddler who sees a squirrel or a duck for the first time. As the child impulsively rushes toward the creature, it flees. Children must be taught to sit quietly and patiently if they want to feed the animals or see them up close. An intuitive approach to hurtful emotions requires a similar awareness. Intuition is as elusive as a wild animal. If you try to grab or chase it, it will outrun you.

A similar approach is required to cultivate intuitive intelligence. This chapter will guide you through a remarkable method of questioning your emotions to discern their hidden and often cryptic meanings. By asking questions — like, *"What is the most important realization I need to learn about myself? What personal growth lesson does this feeling represent?"* — you will receive startling insights, provided you sit calmly, quietly and peacefully, trusting your first impressions.

Self-awareness and Emotional Interpretation

Humans are mostly unconscious — aware of only a small percentage of the mental thoughts, emotional feelings and physical stimuli produced by the brain. Self-awareness varies from moment to moment — diminished by fear and tension and enhanced by peace of mind and relaxation.

Of the five types of awareness — situational, physical sensations, mental thoughts, emotional feelings and mindfulness itself — we are least aware of our mindful attention and emotional motives. Schoolteachers and parents educate us about mental reasoning, and physical education trains the body. Subjects like math, science, geography, humanities, sociology and civics teach us about the world. But emotional intelligence and self-awareness is ignored. The development of emotional intelligence begins with self-awareness.

Increasingly, the word *mindfulness* is used in the English-speaking world to refer to the enhanced awareness we've described as higher consciousness and **Fearless Intelligence**. The Merriam-Webster English Dictionary defines mindfulness as *"the practice of maintaining a nonjudgmental state of heightened or complete awareness of one's thoughts, emotions, or experiences on a moment-to-moment basis."* The prehistoric Pali word *vipassana,* carries a similar meaning. It was 1530 AD before the English word *mindfulness* was first used in literature.

The self-awareness technique outlined in this chapter is a blend of meditation, self-hypnosis, guided imagery, autogenic training and cognitive -emotional behavioral therapy (CEBT). Our goal is to release heartache and confusion by recognizing the root origins of our distress. Expanded self-awareness relieves emotional pain in the same way it diminishes physical discomfort.[45]

Let's review the five most significant principles of emotional intelligence.

1. Emotional feelings are subjective responses. They are not done to us, but rather come from us. They tell us little or nothing about the people or events that stimulate them. Instead, they reveal our individuality and condition. No one can make us feel anything — loved, happy, disappointed or angry — without our participation and endorsement.

2. Emotions reveal their meaning through intuition. Efforts to judge, reason or think logically about our feelings impede insight and understanding.

3. Although emotions that hurt and irritate us are commonly called *negative feelings*, they are not bad. In fact, so-called *negative emotions* are fear-based alerts — vital demands from the brain for more information and greater self-awareness. Hidden within everything that hurts, frustrates or humiliates is a treasure trove of personal wisdom. Positive emotions are comforting signals that encourage us to persevere.

4. Stress, anxiety and fearful tension limit awareness and intelligence. Profound relaxation and peace of mind expand awareness and intelligence.

5. Understanding is the antidote to heartache, confusion and unawareness. It is the remedy for the fear, anxiety and stress that arises to signal our need for greater self-awareness.

The techniques featured in Chapter 7 will expand self-awareness and reduce stress, heartache and confusion. Skilled meditators use these time-honored skills to manage the unavoidable stress of the modern world. Now, let's take the next step.

The Feelings Dialogue Technique

Love-based, positive feelings reaffirm our outlook and behavior. The following technique will reveal and resolve hurtful, upsetting and irritating feelings, like anger, sadness, humiliation, distrust and envy. All hurtful, negative feelings are supported by fear and ignorance. And because *"the best parts of us are hidden where we're most afraid to look,"* we need to confront our fear and heartache to understand and release it.

Read the following narrative a few times until you can recall its general flow during the visualization process. If you prefer, you can record yourself slowly reading the narrative with long pauses where indicated. As previously suggested, listening to the audiobook version of **Fearless Intelligence** may be the most effective method of learning this technique.

Begin by sitting comfortably on a chair, sofa or meditation pillow. Close your eyes and take three or four slow, deep breaths. As you inhale, imagine drawing in strength and power. Each time you exhale, visualize yourself releasing stress, anxiety and tension as if they were oily, black smoke that repeatedly gets cleaner and fresher with each breath.

Starting at your feet, slowly scan your body with your awareness, consciously and deliberately releasing tension as you move through each area. Feel each muscle group relaxing and unwinding. Progressively create and sense letting go feelings from the soles of your feet to the top of your head. Feel your muscles softening and yielding to the wonderfully gentle warmth of relaxation.

(If recording, allow the app to continue to run as you pause for a full minute or more, mentally scanning and deeply relaxing the entire length of your body. When you resume the narrative, speak more slowly and in softer tones.)

In your mind's eye, create an image of a beautiful place of perfect peace — a sublime, halcyon paradise of ideal relaxation, where you are safe, calm and peaceful. Imagine yourself strolling through this bliss, whether it's a beautifully landscaped garden or a warm, sunny meadow beside a cool, shady forest.

As you wander, feel the gentle warmth of the sun on your face and arms and the slightly cooler dampness of the shady woodland. Listen to the birds singing, and smell the delicate fragrances of the flowers, grass and trees. In your body, feel as if time stands still — that there's nothing else you need to be doing, and nowhere else you'd rather be.

Find an area that feels as if it's your perfect place, the most beautiful and peaceful spot you can imagine — perhaps beside a small stream or pond. Sit upon a grassy spot and imagine how it might feel to have roots connecting you to the warm, fertile earth. Consider how a tree, a flower or blade of grass feels to be so deeply connected to the ground of all that grows here. The feeling that you're pretending and just making all of this up is exactly right.

Recall the emotional hurt, heartache, anger, sadness or confusion you've been feeling lately. Allow yourself to feel it in your body as you would feel physical sensations.

Then, trusting your first impression, ask yourself, *"If this feeling or set of feelings had a color, what color would that be?"* As an initial sense of color occurs, ask yourself, *"And if this color had a texture or temperature, how would it feel to carefully reach out and touch it?"* Again, accept your first impression without judgment.

Now, as if pulling a large bedsheet out of the dryer, imagine drawing this colorful hurt into a large ball. Tuck in the corners and work it around in your hands, compressing it from beachball-sized, smaller and smaller, to the size of a basketball, and finally down to a baseball-sized sphere of color that contains your heartache and confusion.

Next, imagine throwing this ball as high and far away as you can, and when it lands, see a great burst of colorful smoke. This murkiness is so thick and opaque, that initially, you cannot see more than a few feet in front of your face.

As gentle breezes disperse the gloomy clouds, you can soon distinguish a character or creature of some sort slowly approaching you as a symbolic expression of your heartache, sadness and fear.

This being will be a virtual simulation, not anyone you know personally. It will emerge as a person from fiction or history, a spirit guide, animal or cartoon character. As a face and figure take form, watch for distinguishing characteristics to help you focus your attention.

Silently and internally, express your appreciation for its presence, and ask: *"What is your name? How shall I refer to you?"*

Your first impression may occur instantly or take as long as 15 or 20 seconds. It may be an odd or common name, a generic title or label. Make no effort to decide on a name. Allow it to occur to you as if you are dreaming.

Repeating the name or title you've been given, ask the character or being, *"Because you represent my heartache and confusion in this instance, what is the significance of your appearance? Why have you taken this particular form?"*

Again, it's essential we resist the temptation to logically choose an answer. Instead, patiently wait with an open mind for the apparition to speak or somehow show you a response.

The third question you will ask is the most important. Silently and internally, say, *"Because you represent something I do not understand about myself, please tell me — what personal growth lesson is hidden within my heartache and confusion?"*

(Pause here for as long as it takes your emotional entity to describe what's going on. Expect to hear a gentle and compassionate explanation of why you're hurting, anxious, angry or sad.)

Follow up by asking your spirit guide, *"Is there more you can tell me about this?"* Again, wait patiently for an answer. Repeat this question after each response until your emotional voice is silent and still.

Finally, tell your inner teacher, *"I was taught to ask you whether you have a gift for me, something symbolic to help me remember what I've learned here."* If the gift you're handed is wrapped or in a box, open it. If you're not sure what it means, ask your guide.

Thank your emotional helper with genuine sincerity, whether with a smile and bow, a handshake, salute or a hug. Watch your guide turn and walk away. Silently tell yourself that you will slowly count to five, and when you reach the number five you will open your eyes, wide awake, with a complete memory and deep understanding of what you've just learned about yourself.

Counting ... one ... feel yourself beginning to gently float upward, as if in the basket of a beautiful hot air balloon. Floating ever so slowly and gently ... two ... you drift up into a clear blue sky with just a few scattered, puffy white clouds. Three ... coming up above the treetops, you notice the horizon slowly spreading out in all directions. Remember that five will be wide awake with a perfect memory and deep understanding. Continuing ... four. Feel the chair supporting you and the floor beneath your feet. And five ... eyes open, wide-awake — feeling fine, better than before.

Quick Fix

The point of practicing this technique and the others in Chapter 7 is to become more alert and self-aware throughout the day. Surprising events will occasionally trigger defensive feelings and impulsive reactions. We have a tool for such situations — a simple, five-step method for quickly returning to a state of high self-awareness. It can easily be remembered with the pneumonic "BRAIN."

The letter "B" reminds us to **breathe**. Two or three slow, deep breaths are sufficient to reassure the limbic brain and bring the higher brain functions of the neocortex back online.

The letter "R" tells us to **relax**. As you exhale each deep breath, create and sense a letting-go feeling throughout your body.

The letter "A" means we must **accept** the reality of the situation in which we find ourselves. Denial does not serve us. An intelligent response depends on acknowledging the reality we're facing.

The letter "I" stands for **initiating** self-aware responses in place of reflexive behavior. Consciously review your choices and take deliberate action rather than reacting without a thought.

And the letter "N" reminds us to **nix negativity**. Our ability to influence others and manage difficult situations requires self-management. We can't do anything for others that we're unable to do for ourselves. Initiate positive goals for the benefit of the greatest number, instead of reacting to what you don't want.

In Conclusion

In his classic book, *"The Wonderful Wizard of Oz"* (1900), author L. Frank Baum weaves a mystical allegory about confronting fear to develop self-awareness. Dorothy's companions along the Yellow Brick Road represent her mental, emotional and physical nature. The Scarecrow feels inadequate without a brain *(mental)*. The Tin Man fears he has no heart *(emotional)*, and the Cowardly Lion is searching for the courage *(physical)* to address his fear of just about everything.

The story ends with the Wizard explaining that everyone already has everything they feared was missing, except for self-awareness. At which point, Dorothy awakens to discover she'd never left home. Her fears were only a nightmare — shadows of unawareness.

Because *"the best parts of you are hidden where you're most afraid to look,"* we must search for everything that frightens us and ask why. What is this fear? Where does its power come from? What does it represent?

As we become more aware, fear melts away, like the wicked witch when splashed with water. The cure for fear and ignorance is awareness — the truth, goodness and beauty of peace, love and understanding.

As awareness grows, fear dissipates. Imagine realizing that every answer you're looking for is already within you, but veiled by fear-provoking unawareness. Then, like Toto, we must fearlessly pull back the curtains of confusion and ignorance to expose the truth about who we are and how we fit into the world.

Everyone suffers from profound anxiety and depression at least once in their life, and probably numerous times. Sometimes the meaning of our desolation is simple.

Many years ago, during an exceptionally low point, I found myself doubled over in the fetal position in front of our fireplace. I was deeply worried, depressed and feeling out-of-control. I was hoping to find some comfort by lying near the fire.

Soon after rolling onto my back, I felt like an elephant was sitting on my chest. I gradually became aware of my unconscious efforts to push against the elephant for fear I'd be crushed. Desperate to rid myself of this oppressive feeling, I closed my eyes and asked my intuition, *"What can I do to get rid of this elephant?"*

Within seconds, an inner voice whispered, *"Let go"* — which, of course, sounded crazy to my logical mind. *"If I let go, the weight of my problems will surely crush me,"* I thought to myself.

And yet my conscience whispered again, *"Let go, Michael. Just let go."* After a few minutes, I surrendered and stopped resisting, certain I would be emotionally crushed by the enormity of my difficulties.

But amazingly, the instant I let go of my resistance, the elephant disappeared. As I lay, wondering how this could be, my intuition whispered, *"You thought you were pushing it away, but actually, you were holding on. It was your elephant, Michael. It was your elephant."*

So it is with any barrier that impedes our progress. Despite appearances, we must take ownership and responsibility for failing to see our way through. Always remind yourself, *"It's my wall. I put it there, and I can release it, brick by brick."*

Fear, anxiety and stress cannot be conquered or overcome. Resistance is persistence. Instead, we must accept our fear and bewilderment to become aware of whatever they represent. Only as we realize the meaning behind our fear, will we embolden ourselves to release it and apply the lessons learned.

In the end, love and happiness are not merely personal pleasures, but derivatives of the Awareness that embraces All Things. We are fragments of One Life, redeeming our illusions of separation and duality. Love and Understanding is the Path to Wholeness.

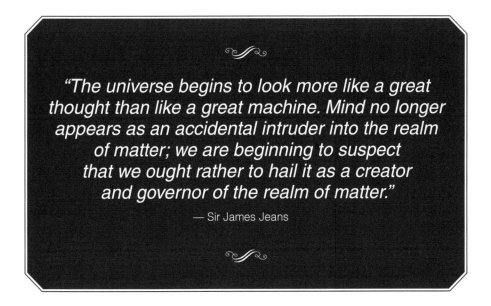

"The universe begins to look more like a great thought than like a great machine. Mind no longer appears as an accidental intruder into the realm of matter; we are beginning to suspect that we ought rather to hail it as a creator and governor of the realm of matter."

— Sir James Jeans

If You Knew

If you knew you are what you care about,
Not just your trains of thought.
If you knew there's more than one right answer,
And have more choices than you've been taught.

If you knew truth is always relative,
And disagreement a matter of degree,
That the only Absolute is the One Life Itself,
And no one is they — only us and we.

If you knew your best parts are hidden,
Where you're most afraid to look.
You'd face and embrace the heart of your fear,
And gain what you gave, not what you took.

If you knew all things are impermanent,
That only Love is eternal and complete.
You'd be living each moment in joy and peace,
Sending Love to everyone you meet.

— Michael Benner
Los Angeles, 2018

ENDNOTES

1 American Time Use Survey, Bureau of Labor Statistics, U.S. Department of Labor, 2015.

2 William Henry McElroy, editor, *The Jubilee of the Zeta Psi Fraternity of North America, 1847-1897* (Leopold Classic Library, Nov. 23, 2015) 184 pages.

3 Christopher Wills, *Children Of Prometheus: The Accelerating Pace Of Human Evolution* (Perseus Books, Reading, MA, Sept. 24, 1999) ISBN-13: 978-0738201689.

4 Howard Gardner, *Frames of Mind: The Theory of Multiple Intelligences* (Basic Books; 3 edition, Mar. 29, 2011).

5 John Muir, *The Mountains of California* (Create Space Independent Publishing Platform, Nov. 13, 2013) ISBN-13: 978-1463714864.

6 Erwin Schrödinger, *The Oneness of Mind as translated in Quantum Questions: Mystical Writings of the World's Great Physicists*, edited by Ken Wilber (Shambhala; Revised edition, Apr. 10, 2001) 224 pages.

7 Ferris Jabr, *How Brainless Slim Molds Redefine Intelligence* (Scientific American, Nov. 7, 2012).

8 John Rousas Rushdoony, *The One and the Many: Studies in the Philosophy of Order and Ultimacy* (Ross House Books; 2nd edition, 2007).

9 Chandogya Upanishad 6.8.7.

10 Tom W. Smith and Jaesok Son, *General Social Survey Final Report* (NORC, formerly the National Opinion Research Center at the University of Chicago, Mar. 2015).

11 Greg St. Martin, *Study: 70M More Firearms Added to US Gun Stock Over Past 20 Years* (News@Northeastern, Sep. 26, 2016).

12 Andrew Watts, *Why Do We Develop Certain Irrational Phobias?* (Scientific American, Dec 19, 2013).

13 Steven Pinker, *The Better Angels of Our Nature: Why Violence Has Declined* (Professor of Psychology at Harvard University, 2012) and Christopher J. Fettweis, *Dangerous Times? The International Politics of Great Power Peace* (Assistant professor of political science at Tulane University, 2010).

14 Felisa Cardona, *ACLU wants probe into police-staged DNC protest* (The Denver Post, Nov. 7, 2008) page A1.

15 Jim Dwyer, *New York Police Covertly Join In at Protest Rallies* (The New York Times. Dec. 22, 2005) page A1.

16 John M. Violanti, *Police Suicide: Epidemic in Blue* (2nd edition, 2007, ISBN-13: 978-0398077631).

17 *"And to know this love that surpasses knowledge — that you may be filled to the measure of all the fullness of God."* (Ephesians 3:19 NIV).

18 Antonin Sertillanges, *Foundations of Thomistic Philosophy* (London: Sands & Co. Reprinted by Templegate, 1956; first printing 1931).

19 Hermagoras of Temnos, *The Seven Circumstances,* originally identified in *De Rhetorica* (late 80's BCE). More commonly attributed to Rudyard Kipling's *Just So Stories* (1902).

20 *"David's heart smote him."* (1 Samuel 24:5).

21 Douglas Harper, *The Online Etymology Dictionary* (© 2001-2017).

22 Ruth A. Baer, editor, *Assessing Mindfulness & Acceptance Processes in Clients* (Context Press, 2010).

23 William J. Cromie, *Meditation found to increase brain size* (Harvard News Office, Feb. 2, 2006).

24 *NeuroImage* (Apr, 2009, Vol. 45:3) pages 672-678.

25 Mark Wheeler, *How to Build a Bigger Brain* (UCLA Newsroom, University of California at Los Angeles, 2009).

26 Tom Ireland, *What Does Mindfulness Meditation Do to Your Brain* (Scientific American blog, Jun. 12, 2014).

27 John Lilly, *The Deep Self: Profound Relaxation and the Tank Isolation Technique* (New York: Simon & Schuster, 1977).

28 Carl G. Jung, *The Integration of the Personality* (Farrar & Rinehart, Inc. 1939).

29 Carl G. Jung, *Good and Evil in Analytical Psychology* (In Collected Works 10, Civilization in Transition, 1959) page 872.

30 Ryota Kanai, Tom Feilden, Colin Firth & Geraint Rees, *Political Orientations Are Correlated with Brain Structure in Young Adults* (Current Biology, 21(8), Apr. 7, 2011) pages 677–680. http://doi.org/10.1016/j.cub.2011.03.017

31 Steven Barrie-Anthony, *Spiritual but Not Religious': A Rising, Misunderstood Voting Bloc* (The Atlantic, Jan. 14 2014).

32 Amos 9:6 (NASB) *"The One who builds His upper chambers in the heavens and has founded His vaulted dome over the earth."*

33 Luke 17:21 KJV.

34 Gospel of Thomas, Verse 3.

35 John 17:21 NIV.

36 Acts 17:28 NIV.

37 Carl G. Jung, *Collected Works of C.G. Jung, Volume 6: Psychological Types*, edited by Gerhard Adler & R.F.C. Hull (Princeton University Press, 1971) paragraph 412.

38 Matthew 5:45 NIV.

39 Genesis 28:10-17.

40 Roy F. Baumeister, Ph.D. defines self-concept as: *"The individual's belief about himself or herself, including the person's attributes and who and what the self is."* (Eppes Eminent Professor of Psychology and head of the social psychology graduate program at Florida State University, 1999).

41 Carl Sagan, *The Cosmic Connection: An Extraterrestrial Perspective* (Anchor Press; 1st edition, 1973) ISBN-13: 978-0385004572.

42 Medical Dictionary of Health Terms, *Harvard Medical School* Alpha waves — A type of brainwave generated when a person is relaxed, awake, and receiving no visual input (eyes closed or in the dark).

43 Candace B. Pert, *Molecules Of Emotion: The Science Behind Mind-Body Medicine* (Simon & Schuster, 1999).

44 Truthiness — coined by comedian Stephen Colbert on his late night TV program, *The Colbert Report* (Oct. 17, 2005), to refer to the illogical, fact-free belief that something can be objectively true because it feels like it should be.

45 Wake Forest Baptist Medical Center *Mindfulness meditation provides opioid-free pain relief, study finds* (Science Daily, Mar. 15, 2016).